T0273517

MOUNTAIN MAGIC

Explore the Secrets of Old Time Witchcraft

REBECCA BEYER

wellfleet
press

First published in 2023 by Wellfleet Press,
an imprint of The Quarto Group,
142 West 36th Street, 4th Floor,
New York, NY 10018, USA
T (212) 779-4972 F (212) 779-6058
www.Quarto.com

Wellfleet titles are also available at discount
for retail, wholesale, promotional, and bulk
purchase. For details, contact the Special Sales
Manager by email at specialsales@quarto.com
or by mail at The Quarto Group, Attn: Special
Sales Manager, 100 Cummings Center Suite
265D, Beverly, MA 01915 USA.

10 9 8 7 6 5 4 3 2

Publisher: Rage Kindelsperger
Creative Director: Laura Drew
Senior Art Director: Marisa Kwek
Managing Editor: Cara Donaldson
Senior Editor: Katharine Moore
Interior Design: Tara Long
Cover and All Full-Page Interior Illustrations
including Spot Art on pages 21, 24: Lea Yunk
(Episodic Drawing)

Library of Congress Cataloging-in-Publication Data
Names: Beyer, Rebecca (Witch), author.
Title: Mountain magic / by Rebecca Beyer.
Description: New York, NY : Wellfleet Press,
  2023. | Includes bibliographical references
  and index. | Summary: "Learn the wisdom and
  magic of the backwoods through Mountain
  Magic and build a magical practice that's
  fueled by ancestral traditions and the
  nourishing power of the natural world"--
  Provided by publisher.
Identifiers: LCCN 2022026718 (print) | LCCN
  2022026719 (ebook) | ISBN 9781577153351
  (hardcover) | ISBN 9780760379967 (ebook)
Subjects: LCSH: Witchcraft—Appalachian
  Region. | Witches–Appalachian Region–
  Folklore. | Appalachian Region–Folklore. |
  Appalachian Region–Social life and customs. |
  LCGFT: Self-help publications.
Classification: LCC GR530 .B49 2023 (print) |
  LCC GR530 (ebook) | DDC 203/.3--dc23
  LC record available at https://lccn.loc
  gov/2022026718
  LC ebook record available at https://lccn.loc
  gov/2022026719

Printed in China

THIS BOOK IS DEDICATED TO
THE DIVERSE PEOPLES OF THESE BLESSED
AND ANCIENT MOUNTAINS.

CONTENTS

NEWS COME FROM DOWN THE MOUNTAIN

THE DARK SHADOWS OF APPALACHIA'S RAGGED MOUNTAINS SHELTER MANY DREAMS AND LONGINGS FOR AN ALL-BUT-FORGOTTEN PAST. The old magics of Wart Charmers and Blood Stoppers and those who know how to whisper away the pain of a burn are supposedly just a memory. Long dead are the Yarb Women who knew all the names of the plants in the forest and which would soothe a heartache or break a fever. There are scores of people, with ancestors from every dusty corner of the world, who turn their nostalgic gaze toward these mountains and coves wondering what old magic lived there, and where it has gone.

Good news comes down from the mountain! Magic never left these hills. It still lives, among strip malls and trailer parks, high-rise apartments and quaint country farmhouses. It lives in city parks and national forests. It lives.

> **Appalachian folk magic never went anywhere.**

Appalachian folk magic never went anywhere. It has not been resurrected. But it is hard to see, like picking out an individual tree from a wall of green. It is hard to see when it does not wear the trappings of witchcraft and magic that we see hanging from every limb of the American pop-cultural tree. The lore of the Appalachians has been claimed by this continent as uniquely American, and in some ways, it is. However, the many Indigenous American, European, and African folkways that came together here to create it, in this sometimes treacherous landscape, have left trails back to their places of origin. Once largely seen as a haven of exclusively Scots-Irish white folks, these mountains hold the legacies of many cultures and their Old Ways and are far from singular in origin.

Despite the best efforts of loggers, mine owners, and enterprising pharmaceutical companies, the rich natural resources of the most biodiverse area of the United States still remain. It is here in these low valleys and high peaks of some of the oldest mountains in the world that wild magic still lives, though it wears different raiment. The diversity of powerful plants, from ginseng to pokeweed, has today made Appalachia a hive of herbalists and healers of all persuasions.

Yet beyond the cure of a tincture of chickweed or a tea of red clover flowers, beyond the weaving of baskets or the patching of quilts, there is something mysterious that hangs like a shroud over these mountains. What it is, we cannot say for sure; it is the Old Wild Thing that snakes its way through the Green River and the French Broad. It is the Very Old Spirits that reside here, troubling our sleep, empowering our workings, and watching us heavily. Perhaps it is the force the Mountain Witch calls upon, for good or for ill, whether they call themselves witch, or more likely not. Regardless, it is one of the things that fills the practitioner's heart with equal parts awe and reverence. It is one of the reasons that now, the author can dwell no other place. For it would not be home.

I was born in Western Pennsylvania, one of the most northerly points of cultural Appalachia, where Hex Doctors and Pennsylvania Dutch folkways were evident in the painted barns and town names. As a person who moved many times, I was not raised in any particular regional culture. But for some reason, when I reached the age when you get to choose where you live, I chose Appalachia. I play Appalachian folk music, do handicrafts like wood carving and basket making, and have found the deepest joy and feelings of home in diving into regional studies of the land I am blessed to live on.

Though I did not get to learn these things from my own Grannies or Peepaws, I did find the place I want to live the rest of my days. I endeavor to share my love of this land and its people, plants, and animals. Bless the people who have shared with me the lore of this land and given me the context and meaning I need to practice my own folk magic amongst these hollers and clear streams. Knowing that my practice is deeply grounded in history is important to me, as it is to many folk practitioners.

> **Bless the people who have shared with me the lore of this land.**

Understanding that Appalachian history is complex, nuanced, and filled with hardships and beauty is paramount to overcoming the stereotypes of our region. It is not a place stuck in time but instead a vibrant and storied place filled with the nostalgic longing of many writers, and the undue judgments of many ill-informed outsiders. Please enjoy this peek into the fantastic, strange, and sometimes gruesome folkways of my beloved home.

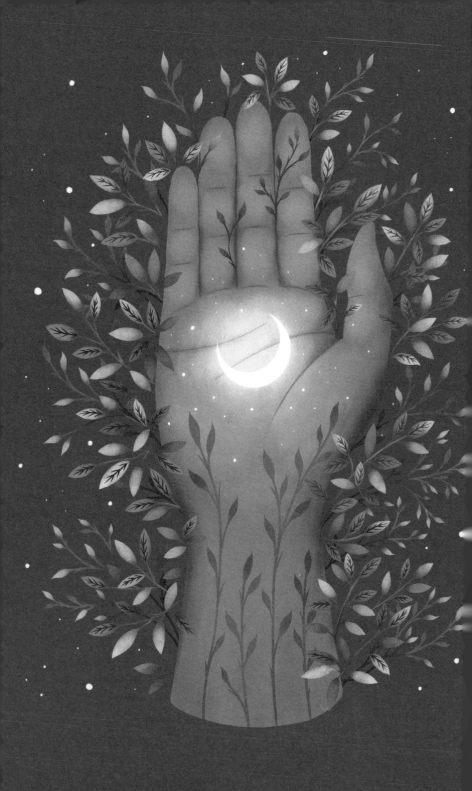

I

THE CALLING

THERE ARE MANY TYPES OF MAGICAL PRACTITIONERS AMONG THE HOLLERS AND ON THE HIGH HILLS. Some are the providers of herbal cures (the Yarb People), some can find an underground well (the Water Witches), and some can even whisper the pain out of a bad burn (the Burn Whisperers). Here, those called "witch" are often good Christians. There are prayers for a burn, prayers for protection, and even prayers for a cursing. You do what you need to, to get things done.

In Appalachia, there is a romantic notion that a witchcraft or magical tradition lives here apart from the ever-loved and ever-feared Bible. But for better or for worse, the magic of this special place is deeply tied to Christianity, the predominant spiritual path of the denizens of these hills. It saddens me to see people erase or wish away this cornerstone of this region's history; for whether we agree with it or not, it is a part of the story of Appalachia.

In the text that follows, when I speak of how things were, I do not mean to say they are no longer this way. For if you ask, you will see that these practitioners never went anywhere: they are just not as often spoken of or turned to for their special gifts.

GENDER AND MAGIC

There is an old taboo that it is bad luck for a male practitioner to teach one of his own gender and vice versa. It is traditional to teach someone of another gender the art of magic. This may harken back to much older beliefs in Old Europe that the Devil transferred power to the witch sexually, though in this context, that aspect has been lost and is not spoken of. This taboo extends further in the belief that it is best not to charm for oneself, and that the most potent charms come from another gender, such as a mother charming for a son or a father for a daughter.

THE APPALACHIAN WITCH
OR CONJURE PERSON

There are certain characteristics that set the Appalachian witch apart. Often they are women, but they can be men as well. Old age, physical deformity, or possession of a "witchmark" or strange birthmark: anything that made someone unusual could be enough to start rumors of witchcraft. Nonreligious people or folks who followed different forms of Christianity could also be labeled as witches.

In Appalachia, the classic activities witches were accused of were cursing animals (especially horses, cows, and hogs), using magic bridles to "ride" people at night to exhaustion, cursing milk and butter, causing wasting sickness, and, in general, going about borrowing and begging things from people to do their evil deeds.

But why be a witch? In Appalachia, a strongly Christian region, to be a witch was to be a servant of the Devil. Yet there were many reasons people chose to be witches in the old stories, from obtaining power to getting back at meddling neighbors or simply adding excitement to a drab and arduous life. Sometimes they were simply born with the ability to get things done with the forces of the unseen.

WITCH DOCTORS & CHARM DOCTORS

In Appalachia, there were, and are, those special folks who learned how to combat the dastardly magic of meddlesome witches. By all accounts, they practiced magic themselves, and were what the modern reader would call witches, for all intents and purposes. Yet in the mountains, they were considered essentially good, if complex, figures. They could give the special instructions and formulae to rid one of a wasting sickness or a wandering husband inflicted by the devilry of other, evilly inclined practitioners who gained their power by pacting with devils. These practitioners of magic are called by many names, but a few of the most beautiful are Moon Doctor, Faith Doctor, Goomer Doctor, Conjure Folk, and Power Doctor.

Witch Doctors could give herbs, astrological instructions, incantations, and charms of horseshoe nails, wax, hair, or other odds and ends to ensure the magically afflicted sufferer could recover. They were taught their art by another community member, generally someone of another gender, as is tradition. Their charms and spells often used the Bible and resulted in turning the spell back around on the caster, all the while allowing for multiple types of retribution. The ways in which the spell was turned often revealed the identity of the ill-willed caster through some physical sign, generally one of pain and suffering.

WATER WITCHES
& DOWSERS

Dowsing, or divining for water, precious metals, and even lost things (or occasionally people), is an ancient practice. The use of a forked stick or divining rod to hunt out underground lines of water or the best places to dig a well most likely stems from sixteenth century Germany, and despite Martin Luther and the Jesuits' best efforts, the practice survived in the settlers of Appalachia. German folkways' contributions to Appalachian culture are still evident in Christmas traditions and a unique system of planting by astrological signs that still persists today. Very often, dowsing was a magic of menfolk, but women were certainly known to dowse as well.

THE DOWSING ROD

The Water Witch's rod can come from many types of trees. In Europe, willow and hazel were used. Yet in the mountains, a limb of green peach or persimmon wood is the most precious for this operation. Witch hazel is also used throughout America, but in the mountains, peach is often preferred. A forked branch is cut green and trimmed to be easily grasped in the hands, freeing the apex of the V to point downward when it is drawn by the forces of unseen water.

In Germany, special harvesting rituals were believed to endow the rod with its power. It was traditionally cut on St. John's Day, June 24, a day significant in the pagan practices of Midsummer in parts of Western Europe. After the rod was cut, it was blessed by the Christian ritual of baptism. The divining rod has a history touched by the hands of many traditions.

WART DOCTORS

Of all the types of cures and charms, perhaps none are so numerous as those meant to remove warts. Among many herbal charms and contagion-style magics, the most common ways to remove warts appear to be in three modes: rubbing the wart with a stone or plant and burying it, scratching or pricking the wart and disposing of either the scratching device or something tainted with blood from the wart, and passing the warts to someone else by "selling" them.

When these methods don't work, there are specially gifted folks out there, usually a seventh son of a seventh son or seventh daughter of a seventh daughter, or sometimes a father of seven sons, who can charm away warts. Some are able to "count" warts off, others can pray them off using special biblical verses often combined with rubbing, and others "buy" the warts from someone with the knowledge to somehow avoid getting the warts themselves. Some people can even charm warts off of other-than-humans. I have heard of a wart charmer who was legendary for her ability to charm warts off the noses of cattle by gently stroking them and whispering to them some secret words.

Wart cures are numerous, variable, and regionally specific. Our very own editor remembers her granny drawing an outline of her hand, placing Xs on the drawing wherever the warts were, and then burying it to rid her of warts. Do you know any of the ways your own family charmed away warts?

GRANNY WOMEN OR GRANNY MIDWIVES

Most Appalachian women of all ethnicities knew something of doctoring. They were largely responsible for day-to-day care of their families, but those women who knew much and could ease the pains of childbirth were sometimes known as Granny Women or Granny Midwives (often not actual grannies, for all grannies are maidens in the beginning). Between 1880 and 1930, these terms were held to be vernacular for midwife, but they meant so much more.

While little is written about these amazing women today, in 1900, it is estimated that 50 percent of babies born in the mountains were born into the knowing hands of a Granny Woman. These women were empowered with the knowledge of plants as well and were sometimes the only medical professionals available to rural or remote communities. Like many magical practitioners, their work was often done for free, or for trade for food or labor. They were the ones who brought their community members into the world and ushered them out. Navigating the liminal spaces between birth and death, which are unfortunately often neighbors, was their place of power, and also sometimes led to their complex associations with magical powers.

Until the rise of the male physician in the twentieth century, they were the women you'd seek out for a broken ankle or a case of the seven-year itch. Whatever ailed you, they would know what to do. Unfortunately, like the witch, the Granny Woman was pushed from her trade by the physician. Though most smaller communities clung to the women they knew and loved, like their contemporaries in Europe and elsewhere, male doctors were held in higher esteem than their female counterparts who had been caring for their communities since time immemorial.

YARB DOCTORS

"Herbalist" could be a good name for the Yarb Man or Woman today. These are the people who know the trees, shrubs, and plants, and the stones, minerals, and substances of the mountains. Most folks knew something about herbs and their uses back in the day, simply because there was no 24-hour emergency clinic, and they had to care for themselves and their families. Granny Women or Granny Midwives often had great knowledge of herbs as well, so the Yarb Doctor and the Granny Woman are hard to separate. Yarb Doctor was also sometimes a special name for practitioners of color in certain areas.

BURN WHISPERERS

Fire or burn doctors talked the fire out of burns. They used a charm from English folk medicine: "There came an angel from the east bringing fire and frost. In frost, out fire. In the name of the Father, the Son, and the Holy Ghost." Or another: "God sent three angels coming from the East and West: One brought fire, another salt. Go out fire, go in salt. In the name of the Father, the Son, and the Holy Ghost." One of these charms was recited in a murmur three times while moving a hand slightly across and above the burn, pushing away from the victim. It is said you can only teach three others how to do this traditionally, and generally most things of a magical nature were taught man to woman, or woman to man. Opposites in themselves are magic.

TO CURE A BURN

The following curative charm was given by Mrs. Sayre, gathered from the Frank C. Brown North Carolina Collection of Folklore:

1. To "blow the fire out of a burn," rub your forefinger about the edge of the burn three times.

2. At each rub, say:

(First time)
"Burn, oh burn,
I will blow you to God
[then blow hard on the burn]
in the name of the Father."

(Second time)
"Burn, oh burn,
I will blow you to God [blow]
in the name of the Son."

(Third time)
"Burn, oh burn,
I will blow you to God [blow]
in the name of the Holy Ghost."

3. One should never run to the wind with a burn, or even the charm will not prevent it from blistering.

BLOOD STOPPERS

Much like the Burn Whisperers, these practitioners could teach three other people their magic formula and practice. These were folks who could stop bad wounds from bleeding, or persistent nosebleeds, sometimes at a distance just by being told the name of the patient. It is said the verse used is the "blood verse," or the sixth verse of the sixteenth book of Ezekiel.

There are other verses used as well. Some call upon another verse of Ezekiel, "When I passed by thee and you were polluted in your blood, I said live!" Then the person's name would be spoken and the whole incantation repeated nine times. There are no herbs used here: faith in the cure is the most important ingredient.

Mountain magic practitioners are difficult to quantify and qualify, for they are hard to see in plain sight. The ways that many of us today view magic and witchcraft would likely be abhorrent to someone of a Christian faith, and the lens through which we view magic and folk healing is important to how we choose to talk and share, or not share, about those practices. When someone has got the "knack," or an innate ability to heal or charm, how do they share that information in their community? Most often, historically, we see people gaining a reputation by word of mouth for their skill in healing, or cursing, or finding water, or charming away warts. Self-identification and proclamation are often looked down upon in most folk healing and folk magical circles, yet of course, there are not any hard and fast rules when it comes to the wild nature of such things.

Today some people say that there are no more Blood Stoppers or Burn Whisperers. But everywhere I have ever taught a workshop on Appalachian folk medicine, I have met dozens and dozens of people who have a living or recently living relative who was gifted in these arts. I hear so many tales of distance healings of mortal wounds and men who could blow the thrush out of a baby's mouth with a single breath. This magic lives on, and despite it being of a subtle variety, it is no less sophisticated or beautiful. Appalachia is a place rich with nuanced and complex systems of magic and history, built on blood, sweat, and tears.

❈ II ❈

MOUNTAIN MEDICINE

THE UNIQUE LANDSCAPE OF AN AREA SHAPES ITS MEDICINE.
The Southern Appalachian landscape is notoriously
mountainous and damp. It is no surprise then that its folk
medicine formed among the dense woodlands, humid air, and
rocky terrain that harbored malaria, numerous parasites,
and oft-broken bones. Aside from prayers, herbs (or yarbs, as
they were often called in the old days) are the foundation of
healing and health in Appalachian folk magic and medicine.

While folk medicine is defined as traditional healing knowledge passed down orally from one generation to the next, it is not just for recording and then placing up on the shelf as a curiosity. It is true some remedies are not effective, and a few are even downright dangerous, but many folk remedies in Appalachia are still useful, easy, affordable, and safe. Folk medicine does not stand still in time, and today, this living tradition continues to grow and change as the people who heal with their hands continue to make and use the medicines of the mountains.

THE LANDSCAPE

Appalachia is the highland region of the eastern Appalachian mountain chain, stretching from Pennsylvania to Alabama. Ethnobotanical knowledge is widespread in Appalachia because at one time, for survival, most people in the region relied upon a working understanding of the useful plants that surrounded them. Appalachians have a long history of eking out a living from the forests and fields. Wildcrafting plants, or root digging as it is more commonly known in the region, was once an important part of the rural Appalachian economy. Appalachia has 1,100 plants that have been identified as having medicinal uses, displaying the wide availability of useful botanicals in the region. The broad diversity of flora in Appalachia is one of its many treasures.

In ancient history, during the Paleozoic era, the Appalachians existed as a large mountain chain. Interestingly, they have been relatively geologically stable since that era, which provided the necessary time for complex evolutionary processes to proceed within the plant communities that came to reside here. As the Pleistocene glaciers advanced in subsequent epochs, these relatively stable mountains—with their mesic, or moist, forests—acted as refuges for plants fleeing colder, drier climatic conditions. The Appalachians harbored a wide variety of microclimates during this time, much like they do today. This allowed the mountains to act as refuges for cold-adapted plant species, such as bog plants like cranberries, as the glaciers retreated.

The varying terrain and elevational gradients of the Appalachian Mountains are usually regarded as separate ecosystems. The temperature, moisture, and soils of each elevational area offer unique challenges for each plant species to overcome for survival, limiting what types can thrive. These elevational changes allow for the large variety in the types of forest communities we find. The mixed oak forest is found at lower elevations, between 800 and 3,000 feet (244 to 914 m). Higher up, we find the old-growth cove forests at mid-elevations. This unique geographical history has allowed for some of the unparalleled topography and biota of this area.

THE ROOTS OF APPALACHIAN MEDICINE

Today's mountain medicine has early roots in the 1500s, with the arrival of the Spanish and the African people they had enslaved. The Spanish arrived with a medicine system founded upon the concept of the four humors. These beliefs were further influenced by the largely West African enslaved peoples who also brought with them their own diverse healing traditions and worldviews.

The cultures from Europe which came to have the largest presence in these mountains, and perhaps the greatest influence on the folk beliefs here, were by number: the English, Scots-Irish, and the Scottish. Scots-Irish and British colonists and their contributions to Appalachian culture are therefore often the focus of conversations about the area's medicine and music. However, it was not until later that they arrived in Appalachia and began the process of cultural exchange with their own healing methods, as with astrology, biblical prayer, and spiritual-medical actions.

There are many cultural components to the story of Appalachia. For example, Native American influence in Appalachian folk medicine is marked and distinct. There were numerous tribes present in the mountains throughout colonization, and some tribes believed that achieving health depended on one's place within a natural system. There were ways to fall out of balance and find oneself trapped in sickness. Despite the racial tensions, the land was the great equalizer. There is much debate about how much plant and healing knowledge Indigenous people willingly shared with the colonists. There was certainly some exchange, but as time went on, the uses of plants and animals and even spiritual practices were forcibly extracted from the Indigenous peoples, just like coal from the mountainsides.

Indigenous knowledge of Appalachia was the result of thousands and thousands of years of cohabitation and coevolution. Their deep, ancestral knowing of the landscape must have stood out starkly to the newly arrived Europeans who had long since felt a sort of severance from their own historic lands and folkways. The settlers could not totally discount the knowledge and experience of the Indigenous people they encountered. For this very reason, no matter what prejudices the European colonists arrived with, Indigenous folkways and knowledge were vital to their survival and left a large mark on Appalachian folk culture.

Enslavement and the treatment of African peoples throughout Appalachian history directly affected their contributions to Appalachian folk magic. Often, literature and academia deemphasize the African influence on this magical system. Yet it is vital to look at these sources critically: who wrote these accounts? What biases did they have? What did they see as valuable? Contrary to these sources, a myriad of African spiritual practices and herbalism are ever present in Appalachian magic. To me, it is not a question of whether these influences are present or not; it is a question of how to discover them.

We can still see the West African fingerprint on Appalachian folk magic. One core belief is that spirits can cause illness. The idea that living out of balance with other people and one's environment could cause illness was shared between many West African cultures and Native American tribes, which allowed for more ready blending of certain beliefs.

The ways that folk magic was shared between enslaved people and white colonists is complex, and changed dramatically over the years from the Spanish arrival until after Emancipation. Europeans were fascinated by African people, but they also exotified, feared, and dehumanized them. As a result, white settlers honored and upheld certain African practitioners of folk magic and medicine, while discrediting others as ineffective, heathen, or evil. This dynamic was heavily influenced by location, background, and class.

There are many different tribal groups and cultures that make up what is known as "African" in Appalachia, Sadly, due to poor recordkeeping and historical inattention, it is difficult to say exactly what each of these groups contributed. However, it is certain that with them came more practices surrounding the inherent power of the land and the sacredness of the landscape. One could argue that the final mixing of European, Indigenous, and African beliefs occurred in the post-Civil War South, where many colonists lost their wealth and class lines blurred. This caused folk healing methods to cross not only race lines but class lines as well.

Certain books also had a tremendous effect on the formation of Appalachian folk magic. A few that had wide circulation throughout Appalachia, like William Buchan's 1794 book *Every Man His Own Doctor*, Dr. John C. Gunn's *Domestic Medicine or Poor Man's Friend*, and English translations of a German charm book, John George Hohman's *Long Hidden Friend*. Their remedies and influence were detectable in many different areas of Appalachia, and still are.

FOLK MEDICAL KNOWLEDGE

The following beliefs and healing ways are characteristic of Appalachian folk medicine as defined by renowned Appalachian herbalist Phyllis Light of Alabama. Disease is believed to originate from damp, dirt, cold, heat, and pathological invaders, spiritual transgressions, and magic. In Appalachian folk medicine, blood is seen as the most important part of the body, especially when it comes to maintaining health. This is because blood is the carrier of the damp, cold, and heat that can harm the body. In this system, to be healthy, the blood must be clean. You can think of the folk idea of this blood system as similar to the flow of sap in trees. Like sap, blood is even affected by the weather. It sweetens and thickens as weather gets cooler, which is why spring tonics are so important in this medicine tradition. Spring cleaning is important to rid the thick blood of winter stagnation.

While there is no one way to speak of, learn about, or teach folk medical theory, it is sometimes said that this knowledge is cast into two systems: *personalistic* and *naturalistic*. Personalistic theory means illness can be caused by a thing or person rather than a system out of balance or systemic, impersonal causes of illness. This essentially means a violation of certain taboos could lead to illness. One can see this in folk medical beliefs all over the world, and I believe it is these shared experiences that allow for the mixing of folk belief so freely in Appalachia, as many of the cultures arrived on the shores here already holding beliefs like these.

THE APPALACHIAN FOLK BLOOD SYSTEM

There are four states of blood grouped into two oppositional sets: high vs. low and thick vs. thin. These states of blood represent four states of folk illnesses.

High Blood: Most likely derived from humoral medicine, this refers to blood volume, not pressure. The symptoms of high blood were headache, nosebleed, flushed face, nausea, and dizziness. Bloodletting and leeches were used to cure this, but eventually treatments to "cut the blood," like drinking wild cherry or sassafras root bark and eating garlic and onions, took precedence.

Low Blood: This folk blood condition refers to the idea that there was too little blood or that the blood lacked vital nutrients. The symptoms were fatigue, dizziness, pale complexion, and listlessness. Some believed that blood rises and falls with the seasons, meaning that you were more likely to be anemic on weak winter food, and in spring, a good tonic would revive you.

Thick Blood: Maintaining normal blood viscosity was thought to be critically related to good health. Older folks thought it made one more susceptible to stroke and heart attack if you had thick blood.

Thin Blood: You would be thought to have thin blood if you were easy to bruise, had slow-healing sores, or were older. The older you got, the thinner the blood. This would be helped by eating more meat, eggs, leafy greens, bread, and milk.

HUMORAL THEORY

As discussed in chapter one, there are unique health practitioners in Appalachia: Thrush Doctors, Wart Doctors, Blood Stoppers, Goiter Rubbers, and Burn Doctors, among others. These arts are a combination of humoral pathology and the miasmic and atmospheric theories which were prevalent in the nineteenth century. Humoral theory is credited as being developed by the Greeks. It involves the balance of four humors: blood, phlegm, black bile, and yellow bile, which represent heat, cold, dry, and moist, respectively. These humors have a sort of balance which is subject to the effects of the changes in season. Winter causes phlegm, and in summer, the blood increases. There is a hot and cold dichotomy that also exists in Appalachian folk medicine, much like in Traditional Chinese and Kampo medicine in China and Japan.

MIASMIC THEORY

Miasmic theory involves the idea that putrid vapors from nasty substances can cause illness. Things like rotting game, bogs and mires, and waste areas could create these invisible clouds of illness. The cures for such illnesses are largely categorized as heroic therapies. These are things like purging, bloodletting, scarification, leeches, and cupping. In Appalachia, many illnesses are believed to have been caused by fluctuations in blood volume (high vs. low), viscosity (thick vs. thin), or waste or sugar in the blood (sweetness). These ideas of blood that can become defiled through certain actions or seasonal changes, are often linked with ideas of miasmic theory as well as the idea of autointoxication (belief that you can poison yourself by not moving the bowels often enough). Many of the remedies and herbs used in Appalachian folk medicine revolve around these ideas of cleansing, moving, and affecting the blood.

MAGICAL REMEDIES

Aside from herbs, minerals, and animal substances used in cures, there are also magical remedies in Appalachian folk medicine. The magical remedies are based on sympathetic magic, which means "like affects like." The number three figures extensively, as well as its multiple nine, perhaps due to the influence of the Holy Trinity. Many charms or rituals are performed three times. Transference magic is also observed in certain charms, for it is believed that illness can be transferred to objects or other people. The color red also prominently features in many cures, often as a red flannel, for red is the color of blood and vitality, the color of life.

ASTROLOGY

Astrological influences—like certain moon phases or even the time of day, like sunrise or sunset—may be considered before performing certain cures. Individual plants and organs are also associated with the zodiac. Many of these specific astrological ideas came directly from the mystic Christian faiths of Germans—who arrived in Appalachia after fleeing religious persecution in Germany—and Native American beliefs.

BOTANICAL HEALING

Appalachia may be the most biodiverse region in the United States. This means there are more medicinal and edible plants, trees, and shrubs here than in many other places. This may have led to a common belief that the environment is essentially a benevolent and healthful place to be: due to the fine climate, diverse botany, and many water features and springs, the mountains were viewed as an essentially healing landscape by both Native and settler folks alike.

Residents commonly gathered plants like ginseng, goldenseal, wild cherry, or sassafras to sell to crude drug manufacturers. Prior to World War II, root digging was an important part of the rural Appalachian economy. This is still practiced today in some areas. The author has spoken with a neighbor in his sixties in Madison County, North Carolina, who harvested bloodroot to make extra money as a boy and got twelve dollars per coffee can full of dried root. The environmental destruction of the Appalachian Mountains by extractive industries like coal mining, fracking, and clear-cut forestry threatens this culturally significant wildcrafting, as does overharvesting of sensitive species like ginseng. S. B. Penick and Company, once one of the major suppliers of crude drugs to the world market, said in the late 1920s that 85 percent of American drugs were sourced from the Appalachian region.

Appalachia has 1,100 plants which have been identified as having medicinal uses, but there are about 90 to 100 plants that people largely relied upon. Some of the most common were apple, catnip, corn, mullein, onion, poke, slippery elm, sorghum, tobacco, and walnut.

THE TONIC TRADITION

Tonics were used to treat everything from digestive disorders to gout and sore eyes to skin problems and liver ailments. A "tonic" is a type of preventative medicinal substance, usually taken as a drink that would promote health and high energy. They were usually a strong tea or decoction (where the herbs, roots, or barks are boiled rather than just steeped), sweetened to taste with sugar or honey. Spring greens such as wild asparagus, dandelions (*Taraxacum officinalis*), dock (*Rumex spp.*), poke (*Phytolacca americana*), wild onion (*Allium spp.*), ramps (*Allium tricoccum*), and nettles (*Urtica dioica*), could also have a tonic or purifying effect. Even the juice of certain plants, like cleavers (*Gallium spp.*), or goosegrass as it was more commonly known in the South, was seen as a blood purifier.

Certain chemicals like turpentine and sulfur had many uses in Appalachian folk medicine and were touted as fine tonics. A tonic of molasses and sulfur was arguably one of the most popular in the eighteenth century. Tonics were thought to move the slow winter blood in spring, and there were many traditional plant medicines taken and prepared during this season, though in some cases they might be used throughout the year. Spring was the most popular time to ingest and brew tonics, due to the aforementioned Appalachian folk medicine concern with blood.

SPRING TONIC SALAD

Note: Always ensure correct identification before consuming a new plant.

Harvest a handful each of:
Dandelion greens
Wild onion grass
Chickweed greens

Harvest a few sprigs each of:
Alehoof (*Glechoma hederaca*)
Dead nettle greens (*Lamium purpureum*)

1. Rinse and chop the wild greens very finely and add to a bowl.

2. Add a few bits of red clover (*Trifolium pratense*) flowers as a lovely garnish.

3. To make a dressing, in a small jar with a tight-fitting lid, combine 2 tablespoons of olive oil, 2 tablespoons of raw apple cider vinegar, 3 cloves of finely chopped raw garlic, and a hearty sprinkle of salt. Shake this well and dress your wild salad.

Aside from drinking brews, one could also eat tonics. There are a variety of spring tonic food practices, such as eating a mess of poke, branch lettuce (*Saxifraga micranthidifolia*), and watercress (*Nasturtium officinale*). Eating nourishing meals of plentiful early spring greens is a great way to engage with the practice of tonics today. Things like chickweed (*Stellaria media*), hairy bittercress (*Cardamine hirsuta*), and dandelion greens make wonderful bases to tonic meals, or when macerated in vinegar, tonic salad dressings. Drinking water in which iron nails had been soaked and simply cooking in cast iron were two more culinary tonics. While cooking in cast iron is a lovely thing to do today, I would not suggest drinking nail water—some practices are best left as curiosities.

Bitter herbs make up the other class of spring tonics; the very fact that they were strongly flavored was seen as evidence of their power. An example of a tonic from Kentucky was one made from white pine bark (*Pinus strobus*), yellow dock (*Rumex crispus*), sarsaparilla, goldenseal (*Hydrastis canadensis*), mayapple root (*Podophyllum peltatum*), apple bark (*Malus spp.*), poplar bark (*Liriodendron tulipifera*), bear paw root (*Dryopteris filix-mas*), peppermint (*Mentha × piperita*), and mullein (*Verbascum thapsus*). This was a true mix of native and introduced plants with many highly bitter ingredients. Plants didn't have to have a strong bitter flavor, for some of the tastiest tonics brewed as teas or decoctions were sassafras (*Sassafras albidum*), spicebush (*Lindera benzoin*), cherry bark (*Prunus serotina*), and black or sweet birch (*Betula lenta*).

Tommie Bass, a legendary Alabama herbalist and salve maker, recommended red clover (*Trifolium pratense*) tea— or white clover (*Trifolium repens*) if you couldn't find red— as a tonic to build the blood. The most-used tonic herbs he recommended were yellow root (*Xanthorhiza simplicissima*), dandelion, gentian (*Gentiana spp.*), and goldenseal (*Hydrastis canadensis*), all strong bitters. Tommie Bass's tonic has angelico or boar hog root (*Ligusticum canadense*), yellow root, boneset (*Eupatorium perfoliatum*), wild cherry bark, cayenne pepper (*Capsicum annuum*), and sometimes ginseng (*Panax quinquefolius*) and dandelion.

> **Some mountaineers used alcohol tonics as a means of getting around temperance.**

Not all tonics were geared toward digestive health, however. Tommie Bass had a tonic to calm the nerves which contained maypop (*Passiflora incarnata*), sage (*Salvia officinalis*), peppermint, skullcap (*Scutellaria spp.*), and peach leaves (*Prunus persica*). Many tonics involved water or vinegar as a menstruum, but whiskey was also an oft-used ingredient. Noted folklorist Doug Elliott writes that some mountaineers used alcohol tonics as a means of getting around temperance.

Like bitter roots, astringent barks were also commonly employed as tonics. Wild cherry bark, dogwood bark, and sassafras roots were combined and boiled to make a good tonic for the blood. Sassafras, long held to have a plethora of healing qualities, from weight loss to syphilis cures, could also help better the flavor of a brew. Wild cherry was a highly esteemed tonic bark as a decoction or soaked in vinegar or whiskey. It was also mixed with the astringent oak (*Quercus rubra*). Persimmon (*Diospyros virginiana*) bark (or root bark) tea, with enough whiskey in it to keep it from souring, makes a good tonic. These varying mixtures of bitter, astringent, and aromatic plant parts formed the backbone of the tonic tradition.

Homemade tonics were eventually displaced in most homes by commercial products like Scout's Indian Tonic, Hadacol, and Geritol, which some folks still remember taking. By the 1960s to 1970s, however, the tradition of taking tonics seasonally had fallen out of general practice. Today, it seems an antiquarian fancy. However, there is still much value in tonics in our modern practice of folk medicine. Enjoying tonic spring foods or crafting herbal bitters for winter meals are two lovely ways to experience this medicinal legacy for yourself. I use wild cherry bark bitters as an homage to the cherry bark in whiskey tonic of history and make sassafras and spicebush tea to build my blood in spring.

SPICEBUSH TEA

Note: Always ensure correct identification before consuming a new plant.

Lindera benzoin, our native spicebush, sits in the laurel family alongside another amazing native plant rich with lore and medicine, sassafras. Spicebush is dioecious, meaning it has male and female flowers on separate plants. Its unique, papery thin leaves ensure this understory plant can maximize its sunlight absorption.

This delicious tea is reminiscent of orange peel and masala. It was traditionally drunk before tense conversations in tribal council by some groups within the Cherokee nation and was said to not only cleanse the blood but also to enliven the sense of friendship.

1. Get a nice quart (1 L) of water boiling.

2. Add a large handful of finely broken spicebush twigs, leaves stripped off.

3. Simmer gently for 15 minutes.

4. Strain with a mesh strainer.

5. Sweeten with honey to taste or enjoy plain.

Many of the herbs mentioned here are good medicines and do their part in supporting overall well-being through their actions as bitters, astringents, carminatives, digestives, and more. The Appalachian tonic tradition is rooted in the complex history and unique ecology of this special place. With bitter or fragrant barks, leaves, and roots in golden whiskey or tart vinegar, the people of Appalachia took charge of their health and found ways to bring themselves into balance. I invite you to step into the verdant Appalachian landscape and meet some of these abundant and healing plants of the tonic tradition.

III

THE YARBS:
OCCULT USES OF APPALACHIAN HERBS

THESE ARE SOME OF THE MOST ICONIC AND SPECIAL PLANTS used as remedies, both magical and medicinal, in the mountains. They form a small part of the large lexicon of healing mountain plants. Some of these plants are also not from here but represent the unique mixing of cultures that Appalachia is made from. Proceed with a humble spirit in the world of plantcraft, for so much has been lost—but luckily not all.

When the closest doctor was miles away by horseback, the forest and fields were the drugstore. The people who knew how to identify and make medicine with plants were necessary and important people in their mountain communities and still are today. Yarb People, herbalists, or Rootworkers in Black Appalachian communities were and are the backbone of healthcare and healing in places that are hard to reach and underserved. While some plant cures are best left as historical fancies, others are still valuable parts of self and community care.

WARNING.

Before there was a pharmacy, there was the forest. Creating a relationship with healing plants takes a lifetime of care and attention. Do not attempt to ingest any plants without learning from a qualified herbalist. Plants can cure, but they can also kill.

ASAFOETIDA
(FERULA ASAFOETIDA)

Plant range and properties: Widely used in folk magic around the world, this plant originally hails from Iran and Afghanistan. The part that is used is oleo gum resin, which is made from the root of the asafoetida plant. It is also very important in India where it is a vital part of Punjabi and South Indian cooking. It now grows in many other parts of the world. This plant has been prized as a spice and medicine throughout the Middle East, Mediterranean, and Europe for centuries, and was brought to these areas by traders from Persia.

Medical and magical uses: In Appalachia, asafoetida is sometimes called assifitiddy, which is a vernacular pronunciation. This fragrant resin was widely used in the mountains for magical purposes, despite originating from so far away. Hoodoo, a southern Black folk magic tradition, also holds this resin in high regard and uses it for very similar purposes.

✦ Asafoetida is often burned alongside sulfur inside the house of an ill person or at the location of some witchcraft that's been done.

✦ To keep off disease, put some asafoetida in a little bag and tie it around the neck. Two balls of it in a baggie around a child's neck will keep away evil, disease-causing spirits.

CAYENNE PEPPER
(*CAPSICUM ANNUUM*)

Plant range and properties: The magical use of peppers came to the mountains via the chains of slavery. Enslaved African people brought the use of these peppers to the New World. These peppers are said to originally come from French Guiana.

Medical and magical uses:

+ Red pepper and salt in the shoe or over the door keeps away evil.

+ The red pepper, as well as red cloth and red corn, is used to cast and break spells.

+ Carrying red pepper in your pocket is a surefire way to prevent conjuring.

+ In the great fashion of contagion magic, it is said that if a redheaded woman or a person of bad temper plants the peppers, the peppers will be the hottest, as if the temper itself finds its way into the shining red flesh of the peppers.

+ Wearing red pepper in the shoes will stop the chills, as well.

+ If you get red pepper in your eyes, don't fret: the cure is to place your head into the henhouse.

GINSENG
(*PANAX QUINQUEFOLIUS*)

Plant range and properties: Ginseng is one of the most infamous of the mountain medicines and worldwide is regarded as a powerful and mysterious herb. Like other magical roots, such as the mandrake (*Madragora spp.*), the forked growth pattern of this often large, tap-rooted woodland native is almost humanlike in its shape. In old lore around the world, when a root resembles a human, it must be good for every part of them. Folktales abound about the unearthly and sometimes deadly screams mandrakes emit when they are pulled from the ground, and this lore made its way to Appalachia with English and German settlers. Some old root diggers, in homage to the older tradition of magical root digging, still warn that ginseng will scream if pulled at the wrong moon phase.

Indigenous folk practitioners used ginseng as a tonic and medicine for everything from hives to tuberculosis. It was also used as an aphrodisiac. In China and Korea, where similar species grow, there are also magical beliefs about this plant, and a five-thousand-year history of use as a near cure-all for everything from cancer to aging to digestive issues. Wherever this plant grows, it is highly revered.

When white settlers came into the mountains in the 1700–1800s, there was a near loss of this special plant due to serious overharvesting. While settlers did use ginseng for medicine, white folks did not prize the root for personal use like the Native peoples they learned about it from, instead realizing that it would sell for high dollars in the Chinese markets. The roots were mass harvested and sold East until nearly every plant was picked. Today we still feel the effects of this damage done by "Seng" diggers.

Ginseng can be grown in woodland areas with some ease, so be careful not to buy it without some knowledge of where it was harvested and how it was obtained. Better yet, imagine this plant to be a relic of the past until the wild populations bounce back to their former glory, before the sharp knife of the global plant trade cut them down. In spell work, substitute poke root (*Phytolacca americana*) to achieve similar means.

Medical and magical uses:

✦ Ginseng is used not only to heal the body but also to remove wicked curses. To break a spell, mix red pepper, asafoetida, dog fennel, sulfur, sage, ginseng, sassafras, and mugwort in a brown paper bag or a red flannel bag. This can be tied around a horse or other animal's neck if they are bewitched, or carried on one's person to reverse harmful magic. A simpler charm bag to break curses and spells can also be made from just sulfur, powdered ginseng root, dog fennel, and asafoetida, wrapped in a red flannel bag.

✦ If you know the identity of a witch who has done magic against someone, mix powdered and dry ginseng root, mugwort leaf, sassafras root, and henbane leaf together with molasses and the bewitched person's hair. Roll this into a little ball and hide it away under the witch's doorstep. When the witch steps over this "witchball," their magic will be broken.

GOLDENROD
(*SOLIDAGO SPP.*)

Plant range and properties: Goldenrod is a common plant in the aster family, native to North America and Mexico. There are many species and nearly all of them have a history of use as medicine and magic wherever they originated. I use *Solidago canadenisis*, which is one of the most common species in Appalachia. It is the one you see waving from the roadsides, blazing yellow in late summer.

Medical and magical uses: Many people look at goldenrod with a scoff, as they believe it causes them to sneeze. In fact, they are confusing it with another yellow-flowered late-summer bloomer: ragweed. Goldenrod tea, made from the leaves and flowers, is actually a remedy against hay fever and other

allergies. The genus *Solidago* means "whole," which makes sense considering its uses for healing old sores and making whole what was once broken. The leaves were most often used for this purpose as poultices or in salves.

Cherokee peoples used the root of goldenrod as a tea for fevers, diarrhea, tuberculosis, and neuralgia. Using the root is a practice mostly confined to Indigenous medicine, but was later adopted by Western peoples. Over a dozen Native groups use up to twenty different species of goldenrod, marking it as a special plant in the medical and magical lexicon of this bioregion. In Black communities in the South, tea of the aerial parts was used for fevers, diarrhea, and yeast issues. In Appalachian folk medicine, the tea of the leaves and flowers is great mixed with spicebush (*Lindera benzoin*) twigs and aerial parts of boneset (*Eupatorium perfoliatum*) for colds and flus.

If you look at the stalks in autumn, there are often circular growths along the slender stems. These are called galls, which form from a grub living inside the stalks. These strange growths were carried to prevent rheumatic pain. Known in Appalachia as "rheumaty-buds," these little galls were cruelly believed to only be effective as long as the little bug was still alive inside.

BLACKBERRY
(*RUBUS SPP.*)

Plant range and properties: Blackberries grow throughout the northern parts of the world, and Appalachia is no exception. Blackberries, both native and invasive species, grow thick in old fields and on forest edges. Bramble patches, while pesky to move through when trampling about looking for herbs, are home to one of the most well-loved medicinal and magical plants in the mountains. The blackberry's sharp thorns and sweet fruit position it at the gateway of gentle and fierce.

Medical and magical uses: According to the legendary southern folk herbalist Tommie Bass of Alabama, next to peach leaves, no other herb has such a distinguished use in the South. The high tannin content of blackberry roots and leaves makes them useful for skin ailments, sores, sore throats, and vomiting. They shine as a remedy for diarrhea and dysentery, or the "summer complaint" as it was once known, especially the tea made from the roots.

+ To make blackberry-root tea, add a teacup full of roots to a quart (1 L) of water and boil for 20 minutes. Take a swallow of the tea every time you have to run to the restroom.

+ You can also make tea from the rest of the plant, using one teaspoon of dried leaves or fresh or dried green fruits to one cup of water.

+ Blackberry jam and even wine made from the berries are also old remedies for "the trots."

This thorny plant is involved in one of our most curious healing magics, the act of "passing through." This may be a remnant of the notion of purification of blood guilt in ancient times. In this ritual, individuals or groups passed under gates or yokes, which stripped them of an attaching stigma. A stand of blackberry briars was made to resemble a passageway by burying the exploratory shoots of these prolific vining plants. The buried shoots would take root to form a true and natural tunnel. This circular space was then used magically as a portal to "pass through" sick children, people, and objects to cure them. Passing through rituals could also use horse collars, holes in trees, white oak sapling splits, and even the belly of a standing horse.

+ In one North Carolina tradition, to cure whooping cough, place the diseased person under a briar whose end has taken root in the ground, and they will be cured.

+ A similar cure for a child or adult with whooping cough can be effected by having the patient crawl under the bush three times forward and back.

JIMSONWEED, DATURA
(DATURA STRAMONIUM)

Note: This plant can be deadly. *Datura contains tropane alkaloids, hyoscyamine, scopolamine, and atropine. Datura is sometimes sought after as a hallucinogen, but it is not intended for this purpose and can cause permanent psychosis or psychiatric disruption. This is due to the fact that determining the amount of alkaloids in each plant is impossible without scientific analysis. Do not handle this plant with bare hands or carelessly, and never ingest.*

Plant range and properties: This plant has debatable botanical origins, but everywhere it grows it has been regarded as a powerful and dangerous beauty. Known as datura in most places, in Appalachia it is most commonly called jimsonweed. This is due to a story from Jamestown, Virginia, in which a cook mistook the plant for an edible green from his home country and poisoned his fellow men at the settlement. The narcotic and deliriant properties of the plant quickly made themselves known, as the poisoned men reacted to unseen forces and cried uncontrollably, among other terrible symptoms. This incident earned the plant the name "Jamestown weed," which was eventually shortened to jimsonweed in the local dialect. Jimsonweed may have originated in South America, though it is now widespread throughout North America and considered noxious and invasive (though perhaps unfairly so).

Medical and magical uses: There are many South American Indigenous traditions of using this plant for magical and ritual purposes, though the people of Appalachia would not have known this historically. They would more likely have been familiar with the European and North American Indigenous uses of this plant.

> **Theophrastus describes dosages that will drive a man to permanent madness and death.**

In Europe, datura was associated with witches and flying ointments, and brewers in Germany, Russia, and China used the seeds to lend their herbal beers narcotic properties. The long occult history of this plant was not so much lost as transformed in the mountains of Appalachia. There are some theories that "flying ointments," or hallucinogenic salves reportedly made in the Middle Ages to give witches "spirit flight" during their Sabbaths, were in fact powerful pain ointments used by healers and herb people to soothe arthritic joints. Cherokee folk medicine throughout Appalachia employed teas made from these leaves for external pain, and used the leaves for asthma and similar uses. Some Western tribes employed the seeds in magical rituals.

In Appalachian folk medicine, jimsonweed is used for pain as a poultice of leaves mashed in hot water. This hot leaf mash is then applied to old injuries, swollen joints, and areas of the body afflicted with arthritis. The narcotic properties help to soothe these inflammations. Jimsonweed was also used for cancers, especially ones that were visible externally. Boils were also encouraged to come to a head with a hot jimsonweed-leaf poultice mixed with peach leaves. The jimsonweed leaves were also dried and smoked for asthma, often mixed with other herbs like mullein and rabbit tobacco to open the lungs. Jimsonweed was used in Black communities for whooping cough and worms when mixed with sugar and eaten. The tincture was used historically to help relieve tics and mania in people suffering from epilepsy.

European Appalachians brought with them their beliefs about the devilish associations of this plant, however, and it was often looked at with suspicion despite its pain-relieving properties. In Germany, folklore recounted that the plant was used in brothels as an aphrodisiac. This was whispered about into the mountains of Appalachia, and another name, the Devil's Apple, was commonly used to describe the spiky, poisonous seedpods. Having a large amount of the green, strong-smelling ointment in one's home could be taken as a sure sign of witchcraft, due to these old tales.

MAYAPPLE OR AMERICAN MANDRAKE
(*PODOPHYLLUM PELTATUM*)

Plant range and properties: The umbrella-like leaves of the mayapple dot the stream sides and the low, wet places of the mountain South in springtime. Unmistakable with their unusual palmate leaves and merry yellow fruits, this wild edible and poisonous plant is easy kin to sassafras and poke, with their varying reputations as magical, edible, medicinal, and sometimes deadly. Known also as the American mandrake, because of its comparable taproot shape, this plant has come to be associated with much of the fantastical lore of its European compatriot. The ripe fruit is the only non-toxic part of this plant, and it is quite edible, though legendary American botanist Asa Gray described it as "slightly acid, mawkish, eaten by pigs and boys."

In Appalachia, harvesting mayapple is part of the root-digging tradition. The harvest and sale of the roots of plants like bloodroot (*Sanguinaria canadensis*), sassafras (*Sassafras albidum*), ginseng (*Panax quinquefolius*), and goldenseal (*Hydrastis canadensis*) for medicinal purposes provided much-needed income in an often-challenging rural economy.

Medical and magical uses: In folk medicine, the roots of the mayapple were used by First Nations people in Appalachia as a vermifuge, to treat tumors and warts, and as a laxative. They also used tea made from the roots as a natural insecticide on potato plants and corn. Settlers came to use it for typhoid, dysentery, hepatitis, and cholera, and retained its Native use as a purgative. It was used ground and powdered to draw the poison out of snake bites. Today it is being researched as a cancer-fighting drug because of a unique chemical contained in the roots known as *podophyllotoxin*, which is used to synthesize an anti-tumor treatment. It has also been studied and used quite successfully to treat genital warts. It is, however, a poisonous plant and was used in certain tribes by those seeking to die by suicide.

The American mandrake has been used interchangeably for the European mandrake (*Mandragora officinarum*) since new settlers compared its gnarled roots to the solanaceous mandrakes of Europe, though the two species are unrelated. Its association with the European mandrake is evident in its other folk name, "the witch's umbrella," as it was said to be used by witches as a poison. The human-like forms both of these roots sometimes take on during their mysterious underground lives have fascinated people for thousands of years.

The root can also be used in the making of "alruna" or "alraunes." These mysterious fetishes are simply roots from certain plants fashioned into the shape of a human and used for magical purposes. Pennsylvania Dutch folk magic and belief left a large fingerprint on Appalachian folk magic due to migration. One of these influences was the use of poppets or dollies. Made of wood, wax, or even plant roots, these dolls were fashioned after suspected evildoers or witches, and "worked on" by Charm Doctors and Witch Doctors to free victims from a magical attack. Roots were used much as they had been in Old Germany among the inhabitants of Pennsylvania, and as these colonists pushed southwards, they brought these magical practices with them. Mayapple was a prime root sought out for such magics.

There are many legends and taboos surrounding the harvest of both mandrake and mayapple, from the idea that the plant would cry out if lifted from the soil and render its listener dead upon hearing its wails, to the idea that the leaves would shine in the moonlight and transport their plucker high into the air. Joan of Arc herself was allegedly asked during her trial, "Who made your mandrake?" Some have speculated that these horror stories were generated to discourage the harvest of the European mandrake to ensure certain sellers a robust supply of this in-demand root.

+ In modern rootwork and conjure, the mayapple root is used to make a poppet, or as it is called by many Appalachian folk magic practitioners, a "dollie." This image is then fixed with a paper bearing the name of a loved one and is used in magical workings for love.

+ A single root rolled in paper money and tied with the carrier's own shoestring is also used as a talisman for conjuring wealth.

SASSAFRAS
(*SASSAFRAS ALBIDUM*)

Plant range and properties: This aromatic native American tree boasts unique botanical features as well as an interesting magical history. Sassafras is often easily identified by its unique leaf shapes, for it has what is botanically known as heterophylly, or multiple leaf shapes on one plant. It has the single lobe, the two-lobed "mitten," and the three-lobed "dinosaur foot," as this author likes to call it.

Medical and magical uses: This native Appalachian shrubby tree has a long history of use among First Nations people and settlers alike. Medicinally, its tender roots were dug in the spring and used to make a strong, pleasant-tasting tea or decoction. It was thought to be a blood cleanser and included in recipes for spring tonics with plants like spicebush (*Lindera benzoin*), mayapple (*Podophyllum peltatum*), goldenseal (*Hydrastis canadensis*), and other fragrant or bitter herbs.

In Appalachia, its uses were shared with Spanish and European settlers. It had a myriad of uses to the Cherokee as a tea, for everything from dysentery to sore eyes. The Cherokee even used it for weight reduction, which passed into use by European settlers and is still present today in the folk lexicon. Sassafras was one of the first plants exported to Europe from the New World in bulk, for it came to be thought of as a panacea and was also enjoyed as a social beverage with milk and sugar in European coffee houses. Indeed, it was even thought to cure syphilis and was second only to mercury for this application until it was decided that it did little to stop the "social disease."

Certain medicine men among the Cherokee also used the root magically. They would chew it and rub it upon their faces and hands after being exposed to a sick person, whether biologically or spiritually, to safeguard their own magical abilities. Sassafras was also an ingredient in treating the wounds caused by magical projectiles known as *ga:dhidv*, which are the supernatural missiles of conjurers. Parallels in the Appalachian medicinal uses of sassafras root as a cleanser of blood can be seen here in its Cherokee uses as a cleanser of energy or spiritual contamination. Sassafras has many more ethnobotanical uses, and it is interesting to modern folk magic practitioners to note the correlations between its ability to ward off illness and pestilence as well as to attract prosperity both in its medical and magical uses.

- As an amulet, wearing pieces of the sliced root around the neck was said to aid in the pain of teething, while a bag of the same around the neck could prevent general illness. In a North Carolina tradition, carrying some root pieces in one's pocket would produce the same effect.

- In African-American conjure traditions, sassafras is associated with financial affairs. Placing a piece of the root in a purse or wallet is said to prevent one's money from running out.

- There are also taboos surrounding not just the root but the wood. To burn the wood of sassafras was deemed unlucky, and in Kentucky, it was believed that burning the wood or even leaves of the sassafras would surely cause the transgressor's mules or horses to die.

- The wood had further uses as a stirring stick for making soap in the dark of the moon and to build beds that would protect the sleeper from disturbances from witches and other evil spirits.

- Ships built with sassafras hulls were deemed safe from shipwreck, while chicken coops built with sassafras roosting poles were reputedly free of lice.

HORSE NETTLE

(*SOLANUM CAROLINENSE*),
APPLE OF SODOM, DEVIL'S TOMATO

Plant range and properties: This small, thorned, tomato-looking plant is common in Appalachia. This plant is considered a noxious weed due to its incredibly tenacious growth habits. The roots can reach a depth of ten feet or more, giving this plant a unique connection with the underworld that complements its deadly yellow berries. It is native to the Southeast despite its reputation as a terrible weed. It had many uses to the Cherokee even though every part of the plant is poisonous.

Medical and magical uses: The Cherokee made horse nettle root into beads and hung them around babies' necks to help with the pain of teething. In Alabama, people used tea from the leaves to treat thrush and epilepsy.

In Europe, a relative of this plant, *S. sisymbriifolium* or blue-witch nightshade, was believed to counteract witchcraft, so people planted it by their front doors. Sometimes protection can come from an ally of the very thing you are trying to keep out.

- ✦ There is a long association with witches and nightshade plants. I use horse nettle in place of belladonna (*Atropa belladonna*) for magical workings if I do not have access to it.

- ✦ As far as poison berries go, pair horse nettle berries with poke berries and string them up dry to create powerful protection garlands—keeping them far out of reach of children and animals.

MUGWORT
(*ARTEMISIA VULGARIS*)

Plant range and properties: Mugwort's Latin name speaks of its magic: *Artemisia vulgaris*. The goddess Artemis, also known as Diana, lent her name to the genus of this plant, and indeed all of mugwort's cousins are magical. Mugwort did more than adopt her name: it also adopted her association with the moon. Despite its common nature and plain appearance, mugwort was so well loved and revered in Old Europe that it was once called the Mother of Herbs, and with good reason. In an old English herbal, it is described how Diana discovered the powers of mugwort and two other plants and gave them to Chiron the centaur. Chiron made the first remedy from these plants and named them Artemis, after Diana. Mugwort is originally from Western Europe but is now widespread as a weed and is a very common plant throughout Appalachia.

Mugwort has small yellow to reddish oval flowerets that have the same down-like feeling as the underside of the leaves, giving it a silvery appearance. This silver down reminds me often of the moon, and indeed this herb has had lunar associations for thousands of years, all around the world. It also features sharply pointed leaves and a tall, slender stalk, all of which emit a beautiful and strange perfume when crushed.

Mugwort is closely related to the common wormwood, a plant historically known for its hallucinogenic properties and the famous ingredient in the equally notorious liquor, absinthe. Mugwort lacks the essential oil found in wormwood, however, and cannot be used as a deliriant in the same way. But mugwort does possess the abortifacient and hallucinogenic properties of wormwood (due to the active compound thujone, the same compound that makes absinthe hallucinogenic in theory), especially when taken in large doses or for extended time periods. Mugwort is also discernable from wormwood through simple differences in the leaves and flowers of the plant, which are fairly obvious to even the most casual observer.

There is evidence of mugwort being used in beer brewing from early Iron Age remains (500 BCE) that have been found at Eberdingen-Hochdorf in Germany. The remains also included charred barley and henbane seeds (another favorite plant of mine), as well as carrot seeds. These may have added other delightful intoxicating effects to the brews. Archaeobotanist Dr. Stika believes the early Celtic beer recipe contained mugwort seeds. Mugwort was also added to beer in medieval times as well—hops were not used in beer making until around 800 CE.

Medical and magical uses: In the Middle Ages, mugwort was known as *Cingulum Sancti Johannis* because of its use as a girdle for St. John the Baptist. Madame Grieve extols its folkloric uses and provides a pretty great overview:

> There were many superstitions connected with it: it was believed to preserve the wayfarer from fatigue, sunstroke, wild beasts, and evil spirits generally: a crown made from its sprays was worn on St. John's Eve to gain security from evil possession, and in Holland and Germany one of its names is St. John's Plant, because of the belief that if gathered on St. John's Eve it gave protection against diseases and misfortunes.

It seems that many of these beliefs were gathered from the Isle of Man, as well as the belief that mugwort gathered on St. John's Night would protect against the influence of witches. The root of mugwort was also nailed against the wall of a house to banish the devil or other bad spirits, and braided wreaths of mugwort hung at a house or shed would protect it against fire and lightning.

Bald's Leechbook, an herbal from around the ninth century CE, refers to the use of mugwort to cast out demonic possession by heating a large stone in the fireplace, then sprinkling it with mugwort and adding water to create a steam for the patient to inhale.

The connection between mugwort and midsummer is strong due to the influence of St. John's Eve and the preceding pagan practices. In France, mugwort was worn on Midsummer Day to ward off aches and pains, and in Germany, mugwort crowns were worn and then cast into the fire. Much like mandrake and datura, mugwort carried many of its magical uses into Appalachia through European, especially German, settlers who brought it from their homelands.

+ To break spells, combine mugwort with red pepper, asafoetida, dog fennel, sulfur, sage, ginseng, and sassafras in a red flannel and wear it on your person or hang it on a cursed animal.

+ Mugwort is also included in recipes for witchballs to break enchantments. Powder the dried herb and mix with a bewitched person's hair and molasses to form chestnut-sized balls. If you know the identity of the one who has laid the curse down, hide the balls under the witch's doorstep and their enchantments will be broken.

+ To heal the various fevers of the South, mugwort is also included in mixtures to bring on sweat and increase circulation, as well as for parasites and other pests as a tea of the aerial parts.

MULLEIN
(VERBASCUM THASPUS)

Plant range and properties: This soft and fuzzy-leafed plant is not native to Appalachia, but it is a vital part of the medicinal and magical lexicon. It was brought here from Europe, and Asia where it originated. Mullein was so beloved by Europeans that it was brought along to the Americas by colonists as they imagined what medicines they might need in a strange new world. The plants people chose to carry with them across the sea tended to be those with formidable medicinal or magical powers.

Medical and magical uses: Mullein is used to treat many things, but particularly respiratory illnesses and colds. Mullein leaf tea is a classic and foundational part of Appalachian folk medicine.

Mullein was used as a general lung herb in Appalachian folk medicine. Its bright yellow flowers towering over the shorter plants in the fields made it an easy plant to identify and locate looking out over the rolling hills. The leaves were gathered in late summer and autumn to dry for winter use. Dried leaves could be mixed with other helpful cough and cold herbs, like the native wild cherry bark, rabbit tobacco, and European horehound. Traditionally the tea or decoction (a long-simmered tea) would be used sweetened with brown sugar, or honey if you could get it, to further soothe sore throats and hoarseness.

+ If you have a sore back, you can rub it with mullein to cure it.

+ Cherry bark and rabbit tobacco combined with mullein makes a good cough medicine or syrup.

+ If you ever feel like there is phlegm stuck in your throat, a teacup of mullein tea often does the trick.

+ Mullein is one of the plants used in bending charms to see if a love interest returns your affections. First, you must know the direction of their home, and in the evening, bend the mullein stalk in that direction. In the morning, if the stalk has righted itself, it means the apple of your eye surely returns your feelings. If the plant dies, this unfortunately means they do not share those feelings. This charm was done with many other plants in Europe that feature tall stalks.

+ One of the loveliest things about mullein is you can make candles with it. "Candlewick" is one folk name for this plant, and that is just what it is! In autumn, you can dip the dried flower stalks in wax or fat or roll up the individual leaves and dip them like tapers and lay them on wax paper to set. Light a bit of the raw plant material and stand them in a small dish of sand. They make the perfect candle for an evening of spellwork.

ONION
(*ALLIUM CEPA*)

Plant range and properties: Onions are one of the most commonly used culinary ingredients yet they are also a powerfully healing plant. We have many species of wild onions, such as onion grass (*Allium veneale*) and the classic, round garden onion we see at the grocery store. Both are wildly useful as food and medicine and have a long history of both uses around the world. In Ancient Egypt there are many sculptural honorifics to the onion's importance as a food to both peasants and royalty. The Greeks and Romans also enjoyed onions culinarily and magically, offering them to gods in ritual. All of these differing cultures shared a belief in the power of the onion to get rid of evil and disease.

Medical and magical uses: Onions have been used for medicine and magic for as long as humans have been aware of them.

+ In Appalachian folk magic, red onions worn around the neck are believed to ward off disease. An onion cut in half and left on a dish in a sick person's room is also used to absorb the disease so it can be discarded safely outside, or better yet, burned.

- In Black Southern folk magic, a red onion held in the left hand will rid one of conjuration. A bit of wild onion can also be placed in a conjure bag to prevent being conjured by another.

- To avoid bad luck, always burn your onion skins in the fireplace and never throw them on the ground.

- Carry an onion in your pocket to bring good luck.

- A spell to tell the weather, gathered in Kentucky: On the night of January 5th, take twelve onion skins and fill them with salt. Name each one after the months. Check the next morning, and each month's rain shall be foretold by how much moisture has gathered in each onion skin.

- Onions are also good to cook down into a hot poultice, or mash of plant materials, to be applied to the body externally. Onion was fried in a pan with some hog lard and then a bit of cornmeal mixed in to hold it all together. This hot mash of onions was used on the chest for congestion and colds, often mixed with turpentine.

- Hot onion poultices were also placed on the throat for a sore throat and made into a cough syrup.

- To make your own onion syrup, finely chop the bulbs of some wild onions and place them in a clean, dry jar. Cover them with honey and infuse for three to five days. Make sure to stir with a clean spoon occasionally. If kept cool, this syrup can keep for about three months. Take liberally as desired by the spoonful the next time you get a sore throat or cough.

RHODODENDRON
(*RHODODENDRON MAXIMUM*)

Plant range and properties: Rhododendron is one of the most iconic flowering shrubs of Appalachia. In spring, the beauty of the gorgeous pink, white, and purplish flowers bunching among leathery, matte leaves through twisted thickets in shady coves is unrivaled. In Appalachia, many folks call rhododendrons "laurels," along with mountain laurel (*Kalmia latifolia*), a different but related plant. This is one reason this common native plant is in so many place names. I, myself, live in Shelton Laurel, off the Big Laurel River in Marshall, North Carolina.

Magical and medical uses: The smoke of rhododendron, or the *rose-tree* in Latin, was said to have been inhaled by visionaries in the tribes of Ossetians, the people of the Caucasus Mountains who descended from Scythians. In Appalachia, wearing a necklace of the leaves was believed to ward off disease and preserve good health. Even though the flowers, leaves, and wood and associated smoke are toxic, all containing the neurotoxin *grayanotoxin*, the leaves are also known as "lucky leaves" in Hoodoo, perhaps due to their evergreen nature. I've met a handful of old timers who still refer to this plant as "poison ivy" due to its ability to kill livestock who unwittingly munch the attractive yet poisonous foliage.

PEACH
(*PRUNUS PERSICA*)

Plant range and properties: A ripe peach is a treasure, surely worth its own golden weight in its fragrant sweetness. Originally from China, peach trees were introduced to North America in St. Augustine, Florida, by Spanish monks in the mid-1500s, and became a cornerstone of the Appalachian and deep South folk medicine tradition. Indigenous peoples throughout the Southeast and as far north as modern-day Philadelphia planted peaches and tended peach groves for their delicious fruits, useful wood, and medicinal leaves and bark.

The peach tree holds a story of early colonization as well, a sad and bitter tale. In the summer of 1779, the infamous George Washington sent an army in a raid designed to punish the Seneca and Cayuga peoples for supporting the British during the American Revolution. Washington insisted the Indigenous-held lands be completely destroyed: "The destruction of their settlements so final and complete, as to put it out of their power to derive the smallest succour from them, in case they should even attempt to return this season." These lands had been rich with fruit trees, and many of those peaches had been selected for decades by Indigenous hands.

Medical and magical uses: Though the fruit of the peach seems an innocent fancy, the kernel and wilted leaves both contain some traces of cyanogenic glycoside toxins that are best avoided. Always use fully dried or fresh leaves for medicine and magic.

✦ Peach is the Water Witch's tree. Water Witches find water through dowsing, the art of finding objects through non-scientific means. Some folks use a forked branch of willow or hazel, but peach wood is by far the best in the Appalachians.

✦ The root bark of the peach tree is used for a tea to treat dysentery; however, an important act of sympathetic magic must be performed to effect a cure. The root bark must be scraped upward when harvested: only then will the healing powers it contains be available.

✦ The peach leaves are also relished in Appalachian folk medicine. Peach leaves and root bark were mixed with dogwood bark for fever, especially the dreaded consumption or tuberculosis that ravaged many with intermittent fevers. The kidneys and bladder also benefit from the tea of the peach leaf.

✦ Peach was regarded so highly for healing that the tea of the leaf was even used externally as a wash for hard-to-heal wounds and the itch of poison ivy.

✦ Peach is a veritable cure-all. One can also magically cure a headache by wrapping the leaves of the peach tree around the head.

+ A tea of peach tree leaves is also used as a wash for the hair: a hair tonic, if you will. To make this, gently simmer a handful of peach leaves in a quart of water. Cool and place in a jar in the fridge for up to one week. After washing your hair, do a final rinse with the peach leaf tea.

+ For a crick in the neck, tie a tender green peach tree twig with the bark skinned off around your neck. Wear this all night, and in the morning the crick will be gone.

+ You can also charm away warts with the aid of the peach tree. Cut a notch in the young growth of a peach tree limb for each wart. Bury the branch in some damp place, and when the twig rots away, so too shall the warts be gone.

+ Peach really shines as a nerve tonic as well. In mountain medicine, tonics are an important rite of spring. Tommie Bass, famed Alabama herbalist, made a nerve tonic that used some of the most famous nerve-calming herbs of the Appalachian tradition: dried peach leaves and flowers of maypop, sage, peppermint, skullcap, and catnip mixed in equal parts together as a tea is a tried-and-true way to sooth the jitters of anxiety or an uneasy heart.

PERSIMMON
(*DIOSPYROS VIRGINIANA*)

Plant range and properties: This magnificent native tree has some of the most deeply fissured bark in the woods. The orange, sweet, soft fruits that fall every autumn are delicious calories for the long Appalachian winters and make perfect pies, puddings, and custards. Animals of all types, especially deer, possums, and raccoons, love the abundant fallen fruits. The wood is hard and finishes at a high polish, just like its other cousins in the ebony family. The leaves, root bark, and unripe fruits are all rich in tannins, a group of bitter, astringent compounds. Astringent herbs and plant parts are essential in folk medicine for their ability to tighten inflamed tissues.

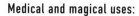

Medical and magical uses:

✦ Tea of the root bark of persimmon trees has long been a vital remedy for dysentery, sore throat, and mouth and stomach ulcers. Indigenous peoples used this native tree to treat indigestion, thrush, and many other conditions by making syrups of the fruits as well as making tea with the leaves and bark. Scraping the bark from the north side of the tree is said to make the best medicine, especially to treat thrush.

✦ Persimmon trees are also magically used to take away chills and fever. If you have a fever, tie as many knots in a piece of plain cotton string as you have chills and tie the string to a persimmon tree. However, make sure not to look back as you walk away, or the spell will not work.

✦ Persimmons also predict the weather. Inside each shiny, brown persimmon seed is a small white kernel. There are three different shapes that lie within: a spoon, a fork, or a knife. The spoon foretells heavy snow, the knife predicts cold that will cut you to the bone, and the fork heralds a mild winter.

✦ These seeds also make lovely buttons and beads for jewelry once they are dried well.

POKE
(*PHYTOLACCA AMERICANA*)

Note: **The entire plant is poisonous except for the fruit of the berries.** *The roots, shoots, leaves, and seeds inside the berries are all poisonous to varying degrees and must either be cooked properly with expert guidance or not trifled with.*

Plant range and properties: The corpulent, fleshy stems of pokeweed and its dark purple berries make this native American plant unmistakable along roadsides and areas with disturbed soil. It holds a unique threefold reputation as a poisonous plant, a wild food, and a medicine. Poke holds a special place in the memories of many Appalachians as an early spring vegetable touted for its healthful virtues by well-meaning grannies. This wild food and medicine is still enjoyed each year in spring when the tender new shoots are under six inches in height. In the Ozarks, where the folk practices share many similarities with Appalachia's, it was said that eating specially prepared young poke greens nine times in spring would ensure the eater's protection from illness.

This tradition of eating the greens in spring stems from the botanical phenomenon of a compound in the root called *phytolaccine*. It moves throughout the tissues of the plant as spring progresses to summer and is toxic in large doses. One could look at it from an animistic viewpoint as the plant making an offering of nourishment to those who know how to safely seek it. Traditionally, poke is prepared by cutting the young, tender shoots and leaves no higher than a hand, and boiling in one to three changes of water. You then drain the water and proceed to "kill it" by frying it in grease. The flavor is lemony and quite pleasant despite the plant's precarious reputation. The berries can also be used for lovely crimson dyes and to make a sort of ink which can still be employed by the adventuresome practitioner.

> **The flavor is lemony and quite pleasant despite the plant's precarious reputation.**

Medical and magical uses: In folk medicine, poke root has many uses. The roots were used in Appalachia boiled and applied warm as a poultice or tea to the skin for eczema, ringworm, and fungal infections. It was also used to treat breast cancer and swollen breasts after childbirth. A strong poke root tea was also the cure for the dreaded scabies or "the seven year itch." Essentially, a strong root decoction was used to cleanse the body of painful, persistent skin conditions.

These uses stem from Cherokee healing traditions and were incorporated into the folk medical ways of European and African Appalachians. In modern herbal practice, this low-dose medicinal is used in the form of a tincture for problems with growths, cysts, and lymphatic drainage issues, as well as an immune stimulant. Dosing this can be difficult, as the plant is quite strong, so please refrain from ingestion without the advice of an experienced herbalist. A salve of the root is also used for cysts and growths of various types. In Appalachian folk medicine, always apply salve with the middle finger, or it won't work right.

The magical uses of poke root are grounded in the Southern African-American folk magic tradition known variously as Hoodoo, rootwork, conjure, and other names. Magically, the root is used in modern rootwork for breaking curses, finding lost objects, and bringing courage to the carrier. Pieces of the sliced root were historically placed in one's shoes to stave off arthritis. To drive off an enemy, powdered poke root was mixed into dirt from the maligned person's footprint, blended into melted wax, then thrown into running water. The tea of poke root was also used to break curses and in the performing of uncrossing rituals when added to bathwater. This act of sympathetic magic could be the ultimate expression of the medicinal cleansing power of this potent root. It not only drives away skin irritations and tumors, but its cleansing abilities are so powerful, it is believed to even drive away a troublesome person.

The berries provide a lovely purple to pink dye when vinegar is applied as a mordant to natural materials. It also makes a fine magical ink, for the seeds of the berries are poisonous, and what better way to write our secrets then in poison ink? Anywhere belladonna ink, bat's blood, or dove's blood ink is called for, use poke berries soaked in rubbing alcohol to create a brilliant poisonous, purple paint to draw sigils and perform your rites.

RABBIT TOBACCO
(*PSEUDOGNAPHALIUM OBTUSIFOLIUM*)

Plant range and properties: This plant in the aster family has many folk names. In Appalachia it is called white balsam, sweet everlasting, life everlasting, or pearly everlasting. This plant holds an important place in Indigenous and Black medical traditions in the South, like in the practice of Hoodoo, among the Yuchi and Cherokee nations, and in Appalachian folk magic. Though there are similar species in Europe, the use of this plant in America is grounded in First Nations traditions from Canada to Florida, and it is a very special plant in Southern Black folk medicine and Hoodoo.

Whenever you harvest or work with this plant, just remember the long legacy of Black and Indigenous peoples whose herbal work made it available to us. Ask yourself, what am I doing to support plant medicine and magic becoming more accessible to marginalized peoples and honoring the traditions that brought these plants to Appalachian folk practice?

Medical and magical uses: This sweet biennial is analgesic, expectorant, antispasmodic, and astringent. Some First Nations people practice medicine with this plant's aerial parts for pain relief and use it as a muscle relaxant by applying the decocted tea and aerial parts externally. The dried brown leaves at the base of the stems are actually the preferred part for medicine. It is believed that the phytochemicals, such as terpenes, that make rabbit tobacco useful medicinally, don't fully develop until this point. It is interesting to note that this plant is often touted as having "little use" medicinally in old books from white authors at the turn of the century.

+ Rabbit tobacco is best known as a lung medicine. Coughs, sore throat, and lung pain were all treated traditionally with the tea of this plant.

+ Rabbit tobacco is used in Appalachian folk medicine as a cure for coughs when mixed with wild cherry bark, sweet gum resin, maidenhair fern, and mullein. Alabama folk herbalist Tommie Bass used it as a vapor inhalation for coughs as well, which reflects his learning from Black and Indigenous women.

+ Pillows stuffed with rabbit tobacco are said to aid those who suffer from asthma attacks. This was even recommended for those with consumption or tuberculosis. It was also used as a tea for whooping cough in children.

+ In magical medicine, people bothered by ghosts were treated with the smoke of this plant among many nations, notably the Lumbee and the Yuchi peoples.

+ Cherokee folks combine rabbit tobacco with Carolina vetch for rheumatism and muscle spasms and twitching.

+ One of the most beautiful ways to work with this plant is to burn the dried leaves and flowers as an incense to rid a space of evil, especially if ghosts are suspected.

❋ IV ❋

THE WORKINGS:
CHARMS & CURSES

IF YOU TAKE A WALK AMONGST THE WEEDY PLACES IN AMERICA, you'll see folk magic in unlikely places. Sometimes, it will look similar here and there. However, there are some things we only find in Appalachia. The ways that people work magic, the materials they use, the words they utter: these are the flavors of a place. Each iron nail, each herb, they all tell a story about the way that magic was born out of the landscape, translated by the human tongues that tell their tales. These are some of the ways that magic is made in the mountains.

MATERIA MAGICA

Materia magica is the "stuff" of magic. There exists in us all the well that is drawn from to "power" a working or spell, but the bits and bobs from our daily lives are the things that were used to make magic in the mountains. Many of these objects and doodads are traceable back to much older traditions from around the world.

HAIR

Keeping track of your hair is of vital importance in the places where people can lay claim to your destiny with just a lock. Clay, dough, rags, or wax can be made into figures to do harm to a person if you have a piece of their hair. They say death charms were made with the hair and fingernail trimmings of a person's enemy. In a similar fashion, if you carry someone's hair, it will give you power over them, and to burn a spell caster's hair will break their power over you. Hair balls are also the projectile weapon of mischief-causing witches.

Disposing of your hair on hair cutting or trimming days is of vital importance, for if the birds get hold of this direct link to you, they will carry it off and make nests. This can lead to headaches, a sure sign that your hair has been used in a bird's nest. The head will ache as long as the hair is used or until it grows back again. If you are bitten by a dog, the hair of the dog is good for the bite. Horse tail hair can be used to conjure someone.

Some people's hair tells you something about them. One of the strangest tidbits of Appalachian lore is that a man who has never stolen anything will have a lock of hair growing out of his hand. If you want hot peppers, they say red-haired people grow the best. If a man is hairy, he's rich; if a woman is hairy, she's a witch. If you dream of hair, it is a death omen, and if one cuts their hair in March, they will surely die before year's end.

IRON

Iron is one of the most magical metals available to the folk magic practitioner. Iron, especially in the form of nails or pins, has long been used in Greco-Roman folk magic traditions, along with those of England, Scotland, Ireland, and many African nations. Appalachia has retained many of the folk beliefs about iron from Europe and Africa.

The way that iron must be smelted and formed in a seemingly magical birth process from iron ore captured the minds of those who witnessed it. From those ignorant of the process came ideas that smiths themselves might even be in league with darker forces, capable of rendering earth itself into weapons that could kill. The blacksmith inspired as much fear and reverence in Appalachian folklore as in Africa and Europe. The water from the bucket where blacksmiths cooled their irons was believed to remove freckles if one washed one's face with it. Iron pots were also specifically helpful to make certain medicines, lending their power that way.

In Appalachia people kept an iron horseshoe over the door to prevent all manner of bewitchment. Iron was also ingested in the form of a "nail tincture." In Appalachian folk medicine, people would soak iron nails in whiskey or vinegar and drink it as a tonic to "build the blood."

Nails are often used in Appalachian folk magic, especially for toothache charms. Right above the sore tooth, the gums would be pricked with an iron nail, and then the nail would be driven into a wooden beam somewhere. As long as the nail stays in the beam, the person won't be afflicted again. Bottles buried around homes and barns were also frequently found filled with nails and pins. These were witch bottles, a magical protection charm brought over from the British Isles. Iron bars could also be used for magical protection, especially of beer. If thunder were to clap, an iron bar placed across the beer barrel would prevent it from souring.

To make an asthma cure, you could make a decoction from wild plum tree bark cut from the sunrise side of a tree, boil it for hours in an iron pot, and mix it with whiskey.

TO CAUSE AN ENEMY TO WITHER AWAY

If you drop iron nails in your enemy's shoes, you can perform an act of sympathetic magic, magically driving nails into their coffin to cause them to wither away. If you suspect someone has put this conjure on you, gather all the loose nails from around the place and bury them alongside a hickory tree off the property.

SILVER

Silver is a protective and powerful metal in Appalachia. It makes the bullet that kills both the werewolf in Europe and the witch in Appalachia. If one has been bewitched, draw an image of the witch on a bit of wood and nail it to a tree. Shoot through the image with a silver bullet made from melting down silver coins. Some say this kills the witch, while others say it merely breaks their spell on you. Proceed with caution, my neighbors.

Silver coins are also powerful talismans against misfortune. Fashion a necklace of a silver coin strung on red thread for an infant to protect them from being harmed by anyone. Silver dimes with a hole bored through them were often worn around the ankles by many Black folks in the South as a means of preventing illness and rheumatism. German Appalachians placed silver coins on bruises to help ease the discoloration. You could also drop a silver coin down someone's collar when they had a bloody nose for a sure blood-stopping cure. You can also rub a stye on the eye with a silver coin or spoon to wish it away.

SALT

This mineral is universally highly magical. A circle of salt protects one from evil spirits and bewitchment. Salt in a brown paper bag with some black pepper and a cayenne pepper is also a potent protection charm.

TO BLESS OR PROTECT A HOME WITH SALT

When you move from one house to another, carry a bag of salt in as the first thing. This will give you good luck as long as you live in the house. Burning salt in the fireplace will also drive away witches who mean you harm.

Folks, especially in Black communities in Appalachia, would use ice cream salt or plain white chalk to protect a dwelling. Take a small container and sprinkle a little bit around the perimeter of your dwelling. If you live in an apartment, a flowerpot with a small jar of chalk buried in its soil outside your front door does just as well. Sand was also sprinkled around the house for this purpose as well.

Salt is protective, but we also know that to "sow the earth in salt" destroys its ability to grow life-sustaining food. Thus, in the mountains, salt is also the main ingredient in a death curse. To sow salt in someone's yard was the ultimate insult and was a sure curse to wish harm upon one's enemies.

SIEVE

Hanging a sieve above the door, or anything that contains small holes, is a great way to prevent evil from entering a home or room. In Black communities in Appalachia, the screen on a window was not just to keep out biting insects, but also acted as a magical barrier. The metal wire must be kept in good order without holes to prevent ghosts or evil spirits from entering the home.

SULFUR

Much like incense, burning sulfur in a house will chase all evil away. Add sulfur to a charm bag around the neck to keep away illness and any curses coming your way.

THE COLORS

The color red is one of the most important colors in Appalachian witchcraft, along with black and white. Red is the color of blood and vitality, which makes it well-suited to healing. This means plants that are red, like red pepper and red corn, are used to cast and break spells. Placing red pepper and salt in the shoes or over the door will keep away evil. Red cloth is also often prescribed as the medium to create charms. Red yarn around the neck will also prevent nosebleeds and cure them. However, if you marry in red, you'll wish you were dead. In Appalachian folk medicine, red flannel is often used to apply poultices or medicines. The use of red flannel is also common in Hoodoo, and one can see how the colors red, black, and white are important in the many ways in which Hoodoo and Appalachian folk magic intermix and intersect.

Black is also especially important. The blood of black chickens is used to effect certain cures, such as drawing out the poison from snakebites. The blood is also used to cure a disease called wildfire, or St. Anthony's fire, a *streptococcal* infection

of the skin that causes red patches. In West Virginia, there is a charm to make someone be liked by other people that used a black wolf or raven heart: "Put it in a frame and tie it around you, that is good. It is also good if you carry the heart of a dove or a swallow with you."

THE NUMBERS

The numbers three, seven, nine, and thirteen are important in breaking spells and in performing acts of magic. The rituals given for how to become a witch often involve shooting nine times or going to a site nine days in a row. In one ritual to become a witch, an older witch leads a young girl to a special spring and "baptizes" her in the water there, each time tying a knot in a red handkerchief and denouncing the Holy Trinity. This is done three times until three knots are formed. Then the convert holds the rag on the unknotted corner in the right hand and turns around three times, calling for the Devil to appear and ask her to sign his book in exchange for witch powers.

The number seven is also significant, as we see with dowsers, Water Witches, Blood and Burn Whisperers, and other folk healers who are often seventh sons of seventh sons or daughters. This likely comes from the biblical significance of the number seven. The seventh daughter born on Christmas day is also said to have witch-like powers. Thirteen is seen as bad luck, but sometimes is used to break curses, as is the case with witchballs (see page XX). It is also bad luck to seat thirteen at your table.

PROTECTION FROM EVIL

It's hard to say if there are more ways to keep away evil or bring good luck in Appalachian folk magic. Carrying the bone of a dead person is a sure way to allay evil magic against you. A circle of salt around your home will conjure it into safety and form a magical ring of protection. Wood from the ash tree, the hackberry tree, and American holly leaves can all be hung in the house to keep out evil. Make a small cross from the twigs of these trees and hang them above all your doorways for protection.

You can protect yourself against witch cats, witch rabbits, and human witches by turning your pockets inside out, or wearing your shirt inside out. If you think you've met a witch cat or witch rabbit on your nightly walks, kiss your sleeve to prevent them from charming you. When going to sleep, sprinkle mustard seeds about the bed to keep yourself from being bewitched in the night. Sleeping with a knife under your pillow is another way to keep witchery away while sleeping.

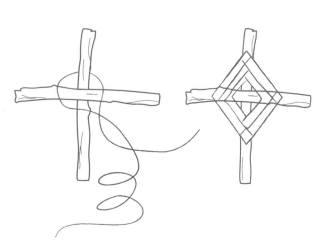

TO MAKE A HOLLY TWIG PROTECTION CHARM

1. Take two roughly equal pieces of holly twigs, the diameter of a pencil or thinner.

2. Tie them with red thread, the color of life-giving blood, and attach them together in the center by wrapping the thread around nine times in one direction, then forming an X by wrapping it nine times in the other direction.

3. Tie a firm overhand knot to keep the thread in place, and hang it above your main doorway. You can also make these very small and tuck them up on lintels or the casement of your doorway for a more private charm.

BREAKING CURSES

Often when we have a string of bad luck, it seems that surely someone must be working against us. Most of the time, it isn't the case, but every once in a while, there is a green-eyed monster wishing us ill from right within our own village. If you've been cursed, there are many ways to undo it.

If you live near a stream or creek, take a glass of drinking water and walk it across the creek. The act of crossing moving water is a nearly universal way to stop harmful spirits or people from being able to cause magical harm.

Images are also especially powerful in undoing magic. Just like having someone's hair gives the practitioner power over their victim, drawing or having an image of someone can help you break their curse against you. Traditionally, if someone bewitches you, draw an image of them and shoot it on a tree with a silver bullet. There are even traditional methods to determine if someone is a witch; if a broom is laid over the doorstep, no witch will step over it.

If you know the identity of the one who has cursed you, simply dig under their doorstep to break their spell over you. Many spells and conjure bags are hidden under doorsteps to be stepped over by the intended victim. Wearing a silver coin, especially a die with a hole bored into it and tied to the right leg, will also surely protect you from curses. This practice is especially common in Black communities.

Willow trees are both mournful and protective in Appalachian folk magic. To keep away evil, lie on the ground and draw a circle about yourself with a forked willow branch. If someone is sick and bewitched, take nine willow twigs and each day for nine days remove one from the bundle. The person will be cured by the time you remove the final one.

LAYING ON A CURSE

I was taught as a child that it is rude to point. In many communities it is still believed that if you point your finger at someone it will curse them for two weeks.

WITCHBALLS

A witchball is often described as a hair ball about the size of a chestnut burr, made of various combinations of animal hair, wax, or certain plants. They are also occasionally called a witch bullet, but this is rarer. These hairballs are crafted to be thrown at victims, either at the physical person or at a drawing of them, with the intention to harm or even kill. Witchballs are a physical representation of a curse thrown. Generally speaking, these balls are fashioned from rolled-up black horse or cow hair, and sometimes even human hair, along with beeswax. In the Ozarks, where these magic missiles are also a part of folk practice, they have been found on the bodies of victims, sometimes even in the mouth. This is sure proof of foul play.

WITCHBALLS AND "ELF SHOT"

Witchballs are formidable cursing objects not because of their ingredients, but because they could also be invisible. This simultaneous existence as a physical and invisible object harkens back to the concept of "elf shot" or "elf darts" in Northern European cultures. It was believed that arrowheads from early humans found buried in a farmers' fields were the fallen ammunition of elves. The wounds caused by these arrows could themselves also be invisible or at the very least, difficult to see. Called *Saighead sith*, or "fairy arrows," in Scots Gaelic, there were many plant-based charms to cure the various strange pains and inexplicable illnesses caused by this "deadly ammunition." The concept of these harmful, sometimes invisible projectiles is therefore clearly not unique to Appalachia, but the fact that this type of magical object exists in these mountains is remarkable. In a place touted constantly in the media for its isolation, the types of folk magic present are not difficult to trace back to their countries of origin.

The concept of elf shot, once brought into these mountains, was most certainly affected by Cherokee beliefs about similar types of magic. Curiously, at the start of colonization, the Cherokee already had an invisible missile concept of their own, known as *ga:dhidv*. These are the invisible supernatural missiles of conjurers. One of the most iconic native trees of the Southeast, sassafras (*Sassafras albidum*), was an ingredient in treating the wounds caused by these magical projectiles and would go on to be incorporated in the Appalachian cures for these invisible darts when combined with European plants against witchcraft and evil.

It is important to note that the term "elf shot" did make it into the mountains in Kentucky. This term was used when referring to cursed cattle, but the transition from flint arrowheads to hairballs as the method of magical transmission is curious, and its exact pathway obscured by time. Whether due to the unique climate of Appalachia or a higher prevalence of exhumed hairballs from animals' stomachs from licking themselves in the hot, wet heat of the South, or some other biological factors, the transition from arrowhead to hairball slowly occurred. It was most likely a complex amalgam of physical and metaphysical factors.

TO MAKE A WITCHBALL TO UNCROSS OR REMOVE BEWITCHMENT

The way to make a witchball is not set in stone, but one ritual gathered from first-person interviews in the book *American Witch Stories* describes it as follows:

1. Find a crossroads in a lonely, unfrequented place on a Friday the 13th.

2. Draw a circle 9 feet (2.7 m) in diameter with a black-handled knife in the center of the crossroads.

3. Lay a small black cloth in the center of the circle.

4. Take an earthenware vessel and, within it, add 1 teaspoon each of finely ground mugwort leaf, sassafras root, and henbane leaf, powdered and dry. Mix this carefully with the bewitched person's finely cut hair.

5. Form the mixture into thirteen equal balls with a little good molasses and flour.

6. Place these balls on the black cloth at the center of the circle, and wrap them in the cloth to store them, only opening it to withdraw a ball when needed.

7. To remove an enchantment or uncross a victim, hide a ball beneath the doorstep or along the path of the conjuror who has harmed them. This will end their power over the victim.

USING WITCHBALLS FOR PROTECTION

Witchballs were not only used for harm, but also for uncrossing a bewitched person. One could roll henbane (*Hyoscyamus niger*) and mugwort (*Artemisia vulgaris*) into a ball with a victim's hair and place it under the doorstep of the victim to keep a witch out of the house. A recipe from *American Witch Stories* calls for "Ginseng (*Panax spp.*), Mugwort, Sassafras, and Henbane, powdered and dry mixed with the bewitched person's hair and molasses. These were to be hidden under the witch's doorstep to break the bewitchment." This essentially turned the magic of a conjurer back upon them, a concept we see over and over in Appalachian witchcraft and folk magic.

The inclusion of old-world plants like henbane and mugwort in these recipes is a clear linkage to the folk magic of Western Europe. When mixed with the magically powerful Native tree sassafras and the iconic Appalachian root ginseng, the recipes stand as fine examples of the unique melding of the diverse cultural influences of the mountains. It seems a logical choice to combine the best of both worlds in efforts to fight these invisible weapons.

SATOR ROTAS SQUARE

This charm is a small square of paper with "SATOR ROTAS" written upon it in the shape of a square. It is used to find lost things and is either spoken out loud or written on a piece of paper. It is very, very old, and not unique to Appalachia. This charm was found etched onto a wall in Pompeii and has been found all over Europe, from Italy to Sweden. While the exact origin is still debated, it is likely originally Mithraic, later becoming a part of Christian syncretism and surviving among various Christian traditions. This means that this symbol most likely has Persian roots.

It was found inscribed on walls, often above doors, to keep out evil spirits and malefic witches. SATOR ROTAS is a palindrome, and curiously, a near universal folk belief holds that the Devil or evil spirits cannot tamper with these special word images. In Pennsylvania Dutch folk magic, it is used to put out fires, keep travelers from exhaustion, and protect cattle from witchcraft. It was especially used by Pennsylvania German Appalachians, written on small squares of paper, and either fed to cattle to protect them from witchcraft or glued above windows and doors in a household to provide the inhabitants the same protections.

TO MAKE THE SATOR ROTAS SQUARE

To make a square of your own to protect house and land, simply inscribe these words to form a square on a sheet of new paper. Roll it up or fold it and secret it away among the eves of your home or barn, or in your vehicle.

S	A	T	O	R
A	R	E	P	O
T	E	N	E	T
O	P	E	R	A
R	O	T	A	S

ABRACADABRA CHARM

This word charm has made its way into popular culture, with many children's magicians declaring it loudly! A possible meaning of the word "abracadabra" is of Jewish origin: "God sends forth His lightning to scatter His enemies," a sentence from a Psalm of David. ABRACADABRA was used to diminish disease, much like the word diminishes as it goes down to a single A. This act of imitation in magic is called "sympathetic magic." As the word decreases, the theory is that so too does the disease.

These triangles were first mentioned in a third-century book, *Liber Medicinalis*, where the author recommended malaria suffers wear them as an amulet written on paper. They continued to appear even on the doorways of Londoners fearing the great plague and were carried on one's person to avoid disease or diminish it. It was also believed to have the power of curing the pain of a toothache. These charms are most often found in Appalachia in the eaves of barns and houses to prevent fire and protect the animals and people within from witchcraft.

TO MAKE THE ABRACADABRA CHARM

1. Make the charm shown below by writing it upon a bit of paper and wrapping it in green silk.

ABRACADABRA

ABRACADABR

ABRACADAB

ABRACADA

ABRACA

ABRAC

ABRA

ABR

AB

A

2. Secret it away, somewhere no one will find it, and while no one witnesses you.

WITCH BOTTLES

A witch bottle is a glass or ceramic vessel filled with odds and ends, from pins to human hair and fingernails. Placing items in glass bottles or ceramic containers and burying them is an ancient practice that is almost ubiquitous, yet these magical protection charms found buried around hearths in Appalachia most likely came with English colonists. One of the earliest descriptions of a witch bottle in Suffolk, England, appears in 1681 in Joseph Glanvill's *Saducismus Triumphatus*, or "Evidence Concerning Witches and Apparitions," where a wizard's curse against a woman is ended using a glass bottle containing her urine and iron nails and pins, cooked by the fireside.

Witch bottles have been used in folk magic in Europe for a long time. Their contents are often different, but the theory is that by using protective metals like iron, a metal long associated with keeping away demons, devils, and evil spirits nearly worldwide, and some parts of the person in need of protection, such as hair, urine, or fingernail clippings, you could create a magical decoy and spirit trap.

In Appalachia, there are many reasons to make a bottle and many ways to make one. Though most of the people who made them in the old days would never call themselves witches, they were using magic to stop magic.

TO MAKE A WITCH BOTTLE

Here is one method to make a witch bottle to protect a household in the fashion of many Appalachians.

Materials
A bottle
Hair, fingernails, and urine from the whole family
3 black straight pins
Candles

1. Fill the bottle with the hair, fingernails, urine, and pins.

2. Make a fire, rake the ashes, then bury the bottle in it.

3. Light as many candles as there are people in the family.

4. Say the Lord's Prayer and the bottle is ready.

5. Bury the bottle outside the front door, upside down, or hidden in the eaves or chimney of the house. If you live in an apartment or home you'll soon be leaving, just bury the bottle in a flowerpot and take it along with you to your next home.

To protect children, try this recipe: Put the left foot of a toad, a bat wing, a snail, and a spider in a red cloth. Put the bundle in a bottle and hang it by a bewitched child's bed.

HEALING CHARMS

Some charms are to hurt, but most are to heal. Magic can seem an art hell-bent on harming, but truly, the reason folks reach for candles and pins is usually to aid someone they love or help heal a hurt they have. Appalachian folk healing often involves prayers, words, and some good plants and bits of things one can find around the house.

MEASURING

Using pieces of string, sourwood sticks, or other objects to measure a child or a length of a person was a way to affect that person in healing magics. Many childhood diseases were cured with this magical healing practice.

+ To protect a child against croup, or upper respiratory infection, measure a child with a stick, put the stick in the closet, and keep it hidden away and don't look at it. When the child grows past the height of the stick, they will be cured.

+ Similar methods were even used for the dreaded tuberculosis infection, or phthisis, as it was called. You could use a broomstick if you didn't have any sourwood handy. Simply measure yourself with a broomstick and put the broomstick upstairs where you will never see it again, and you will be cured.

+ Warts were also curable with this measuring technique. This spell required a twig cut near a running stream, after which you cut as many notches in the stick as you have warts. Throw the twig into the stream and never look back, and the warts will go away as the stick rots away in the water.

+ Flax, or linen thread, was also used to provide cures by measuring. If a child suffered from undergrowth, or failure to thrive, the thread would be used to measure a certain part of the body, such as the head, and then the whole thread would be fashioned into a loop. The child would then be passed back and forth through the loop nine times. The thread would then be secreted away somewhere, most likely in the eaves of the home, to decay. When the thread decayed, the affliction would be overcome.

PLUGGING

Plugging is another magical practice used in the mountains with mysterious origins. It is the act of making a hole in either a living tree or some timbers in a home, then stuffing objects into the hole and either closing it up or driving nails into it. It was not as popular in America as in Europe, yet it persisted in Appalachia. Many types of trees were used in this strange method of healing common ailments.

+ There is a spell to help a child failing to thrive, in which you can measure them by the door jamb in their home. Bore a hole at the child's exact height, right above their head. Hammer a piece of wood into this hole and then whittle it off so you can no longer see it. This ensures the child would grow rapidly!

+ To cure a wart with plugging, prick the wart and wipe the drop of blood off with a rag; then, bore a hole in a white oak tree, and put a peg in to hold the rag in place. Whisper to the wart every night for nine nights, "Be gone," and it will heal.

PLUGGING AS DEFENSIVE MAGIC

To harm a witch who has been conjuring you, make a ticket, or a piece of paper with a specific Bible verse and the name of the accused, then bore a hole in a stout white oak tree. Take an iron rod and use the rod to push the ticket into the hole. That will harm the source of your trouble.

These tickets are protective amulets in themselves and are a stand-alone protection against malefic influences: for any witch up to no good cannot walk forward through a door over which a ticket is hung, they must walk backward, and in doing so, identify themselves, for these evildoers must do many things in reverse.

To make a ticket, take a scrap of paper and write, "Get thee behind me, Satan: thou art an offense unto me; for thou savourest not the things that be of God, but those that be of men" (Matt. 16:23). After this, write the person's name and the three highest names. The ticket can then be harmed by driving it into an oak tree with an iron rod, cutting it with a knife, or burning it with fire. If the meddlesome witch whose name is written on the paper has indeed conjured you, they will be visible in the community with injuries similar to the harm done to the ticket in due time.

✦ To cure hernia, the plugging must be done under the right sign. Choose a stout fruit tree and bore a hole in it. Before daylight, take a piece of cloth from the afflicted's clothing that's closest to the hernia. Put hair and nail clippings from the upper and lower parts of the body into this piece of cloth. Tie it all up and drive it into the hole, then deliver three blows to drive a wooden plug into the hole while reciting, "In the name of the Father, the Son, and the Holy Ghost!" (one name for each blow).

PULLING OR PASSING THROUGH

Passing a person or child through a hole formed in nature was also a potent magical charm. The following charms are from the Frank C. Brown collection of North Carolina Folklore:

✦ "To cure hernia (rupture) in a young child, pass [them] three times through the split trunk of a young tree, and tie the split pieces together again; if they grow together, the child will be cured" (No. 311).

✦ "To cure whooping cough, find a blackberry or raspberry bush whose top has been turned down and taken root, make the patient crawl under it three times" (No. 2721).

WART CHARMS

It seems there are more charms for warts than almost any other predicament in the mountains. Warts can be charmed away through what is known as transference magic. This is when one thing is transferred to another via magical means.

✦ If you steal a dishrag from a mother or grandmother and rub the wart with it, hide it away or bury it, and when it rots, the warts will be gone.

- You can also sell warts for a penny each: simply use pennies, stones, or knots in a string, and either hide them to be found by another who will "pick them up" from you or bury them to degrade. The second option is much more ethical.

- Stump water is also believed to be imbued naturally with healing powers, for it never touches earth. Wash your warts in stump water to cure them.

- If a person is born the ninth son of the family, he will be naturally gifted at wart charming.

- Sprinkled on a wart, newly dug grave dirt is another sure cure.

- You can tie a tail hair from a gray mare around the warts and this will cause them to wither.

- In the same fashion as the rag spell, you can prick each wart with a pin, then bury them.

LOVE WORKINGS

Workings of the heart are often dangerous territory. To bend another's will is surely an evil thing, and these charms are included here as historical fancies. Remember, magic cannot be undone completely, only redirected. Heed this warning or dire consequences await those who are foolish enough to try and win a lover's heart without true passion.

A GERMAN LOVE CHARM

From the German settlers of Appalachia comes this love charm:

Walk to the garden in the light of the first quarter of the new moon. Take a white cotton handkerchief or a piece of cloth with you. Spread it out on the ground and squat, positioning yourself so that the new moon is visible over your left shoulder, and say:

> *"New Moon, True Moon, pray tell unto me,*
> *Who it is my true love shall be.*
> *The color of his eyes and hair,*
> *Show me in my sleep tonight."*

As you say this chant, scoop three handfuls of dirt and place them in your handkerchief. Tie the handkerchief into a bundle and walk backward to the house without speaking. Put the bundle under your pillow, and go directly to sleep. That night, you will dream of your true love. The next morning, untie the bundle and sift through the dirt with your fingers. There you will find a hair from the head of the man you will marry.

- There are many ballads that mention the Lover's Knot as a magical tangle of certain plants and trees symbolizing their eternal love. It is a common practice for some courting couple to find a young sapling of a tree, and to then take a small branch of the tree and tie it into a knot. As the tree grows, the knot gets tighter and more permanent, thus resulting in a permanent love. However, if the knot would not hold or came untied later, then the love would ultimately fail. The knot is both an act of magic to ensure lasting love and a divination to determine its fate.

- To see if your love loves you back, take a rose leaf or petal, kiss it, and name it the name of your fancy. After that, fold it together like gathering up a bag and pop it on your forehead. If it fails to pop, he doesn't love you.

- Simply possessing a lock of someone's hair can cause them to desire to be your sweetheart. Obtaining the hair, however, is risky business. If you sew it into your clothing, the person of your affection will go mad for you. If your husband is wandering, plug his hair into the door frame and he will stop his wandering ways.

- If a girl wants a lover who returns her affections to visit within three days' time, all she needs is a pin and a clean square of paper. With the new pin, she should pierce the third finger of the left hand, and in very small writing, in the center of the square of paper, write both of their initials, and then draw three rings in blood around them. Without anyone knowing, the square must be buried outside at nine o'clock at night. If her lover truly loves her, they will come in three days.

A SPELL TO SEE YOUR FUTURE HUSBAND

Materials
A dark, empty room
A hand mirror
A bright red apple

1. Once dark sets in, wait in the dark room in total silence until the moon rises.

2. Turn three times to the left all the way around.

3. Hold the mirror up to your face, and say the following three times: "Wenty Sarum."

4. Close your eyes, take three bites of the apple and swallow it, then open your eyes. Your beloved's face will appear in the mirror.

- The red heart's blood has long been used in love charms, however dire it may be. Take clippings from your left first fingernail and three hairs from your head wetted in a drop of your own red blood. Tie these into some bit of clothing you have worn, then bury them under the northeast corner of your beloved's home to win their love.

- If a woman wants to bewitch a man into loving her, she may rub her eyes with a pearl, after which when she gazes at him, he will be mad for her. Similarly, she may take a picture of her intended and place it in a drawer. Then she must cover it up with her clothing and she will win their love. If he is trying to go and court another, she can sprinkle salt in his path, and he will return to her.

- Certain plants aid in love magic. Grape leaves that are joined together can be worn under the arm to obtain the affection of the one you love. This charm comes from Black Appalachian folk practice. Hellebore is also used in love spells. The beautiful native sweet shrub (*Calycanthus floridus*) can also be carried in one's pocket to win a girl's love. Sprinkling heart lead or liverwort (*Hepatica triloba*) over a man's clothes will also make a man love you. Better yet, carry some on your bosom, and many will love you.

In Appalachian folk magic, in the fashion of much older pagan practices, the best time to do these love charms is traditionally June 22, which is coincidentally the day after Midsummer, or the summer solstice. This ancient European holiday was rife with love workings, fertility rites, and divinations. Despite the religion of the mountains, this belief persists.

GHOSTS & SPIRITS

Wandering shades are a part of almost every folk culture around the world. In Appalachia there are many words for ghosts. Boogers, haints, and spirits are the most common, but every community has their preference. Ghosts come to be through the slighting of a human soul. Normally, when a person dies, their soul moves on. However, if they have been harmed or wronged, they can become a ghost.

Sudden blasts of both warm and cold air reveal a wandering spirit is near. If you feel one, turn your pockets out and they can do you no harm. Doors opening by themselves, empty rocking chairs in motion, and lights dimming on their own also let one know a ghost is present. If you comb your hair in the night, ghosts will trouble your sleep. Horses, dogs, and cats will also alert you to the present of the undead, through balking, howling, and hissing.

To commune with the dead, eat salt for nine mornings before the sun comes up. No words can be spoken until after the spoonful of salt is eaten. If a spirit approaches, simply ask them, "What do you want?" They will leave you untroubled. Some say there is a charm to gift a ghost with speech, and that is to ask them, "In the name of the Father, the Son, and the Holy Ghost, what do you want?"

To keep ghosts away, you may place good things like bread and coffee under the house and it will prevent them from entering. Horseshoes above the door are always a good idea.

ANIMALIA

In Appalachia, animals held many different roles and inspired an array of folk beliefs. Some animals were necessary for agrarian life, like the cow and the chicken. Others were hunted for sustenance, like the deer and the raccoon. Still others, like the cat and the toad, had a more complex status. Animal parts and bones were prominently used in Appalachian folk magic and Hoodoo in the mountains. Today, we shift our uses of these sometimes-ill-gotten materials for other, more ethical ingredients, but peering into the ways certain animals and insects captured the Appalachian imagination is fascinating and shows the threads tying Appalachian magic to much older and more magical practices.

FAMILIARS

The idea of the witch's familiar is certainly an iconic one, evident in writing all the way from the 1200s in Germany. In a letter from 1232, Pope Gregory IX addressed a letter to King Henry of Germany in which he mentioned black cats, shape-shifting animals, and familiar spirits. Gerald Milnes posits that perhaps the belief in familiar animals lies in older, pre-Christian Norse beliefs about Odin and his ability to send out his spirit while he sleeps, in the form of birds, fish, serpents, and other animals. However they came to be, these beliefs traveled with German settlers all the way to the mountains of Appalachia, where cats, toads, and other animals have come to be known as familiars to the Appalachian witch.

TOADS

The toad is a prominent animal in British Isles folklore, so it only makes sense that the toads of the New World came to occupy a similar place in Appalachian lore. Toads are both used in cures and seen as bad omens. Some lore says that if your petition to the devil to become a witch was successful, a toad would be awaiting you at home, ready to be your "imp." Toad blood was also sometimes used to coat the silver bullets used to shoot at the moon or the rising sun in witch dedication rituals. The toad is also sometimes the witch himself or herself. Taking the likeness of a toad in order to access small spaces is a classic trick of the Appalachian Witch. Even the devil himself is said to show himself to witches in the guise of a toad. Toads were said to be kept like chickens by witches, and one would know a toad egg by its very hard shell. Even the glance of the toad was thought to cause evil.

Yet, as mentioned before, using the toes or feet of toads is relatively common in sachets hung above the bed to counteract witchcraft. This is a great example of many folk cures where something that is perceived to cause harm is used in the cure. We can see this further in the belief that to kill a toad would bring bloody milk. It's a bit like magical homeopathy. If children were bewitched, they were instructed to wear a dried toad toe around their neck. It may be the natural affinity for toads and frogs that especially aligns these wee beasties with children and bewitchment.

Frogs also have similar beliefs surrounding them. Every frog you kill will make your life shorter, and some say you'll even be hit by lightning for this crime.

CATS

The form of a cat is another that Appalachian witches frequently take. There are enough beliefs about cats in Appalachia, especially black cats, to fill an entire book of its own. Many women take the form of cats in Appalachian witch tales to meet with other cat-disguised witches, or even to commit murder. Black cat bones and blood were unfortunately used frequently in curing shingles, in rituals to become a witch, and in many folk cures for nasty skin infections. The black cat bone is also important to Hoodoo practitioners and their rites in Appalachia. However, to obtain this bone is also horrible luck, for it is always bad luck to kill a cat. Interestingly enough, the black cat who can bring bad luck by crossing your path brings good luck when they enter your front door.

DOGS

Dogs are both troublesome and protective in Appalachian folk magic, depending on their actions. If a sick person is in the house, a dog must not be permitted to run about, or the sick person will never recover. A dog must never howl near a sick person as well, for it will be a death call. Dogs, and cats for that matter, will also always know when death comes to a home. But dogs in general are lucky animals in Appalachian folk magic. They bring luck just by following you home. If a dog ever barks at you, just tell them where you are going, and they will stop.

SNAKES

Snakes hold much power, and it is said if you capture a snake, especially a black snake, and eat its still-living heart, untold power will be yours. However, killing a snake is also unlucky and will cause the cows to give bloody milk. If a snake is found in someone's bed, it means they are surely conjured. Finding a shed snakeskin, however, is very lucky, and it is especially good luck to touch it. Snakes are mysterious animals, and there is also a belief that they never die until sundown. If, during a drought, a black snake is killed and hung over a fence belly side up, it will rain in three days.

CHICKENS

Black chickens especially are useful in magical cures, particularly their blood. For the disease known as "wildfire," or erysipelas, the blood of a freshly killed black chicken is applied to the afflicted area. It is also used for snake bites, and the intestines are used, rather than just the blood. The intestines are believed to draw out the poison.

Chickens, especially ones with ruffled feathers, are excellent at keeping away conjure due to their scratching about the yard and uncovering buried items. The skin of their gizzards was also used medicinally to treat indigestion, a folk medical practice illuminating the magic of "like cures like." The gizzards were dried and pulverized, served in water.

If a hen tries to crow like a cock, it means there will be a death in the family.

BEETLES

The beetle is a convenient, tiny familiar that can easily access hard-to-enter keyholes and cracks in the windows. Unfortunately, they are also easy to catch and keep in little bottles.

HOGS

The teeth of a hog are very good charms against teething pain in babies and were especially popular among Black communities in Appalachia. There is a special bone in the head of the hog that naturally has a hole through it. This miraculous bone was used on a bit of thread and wrapped up in a white muslin bag by Black mothers to magically aid their babies in the pains of teething.

If the hogs take to fighting, it means a storm is sure to come.

WOLVES

From the German-Swiss tradition, there comes the belief that wearing a wolf's tooth will grant you protection.

V

SEASONAL LORE & MOUNTAIN ASTROLOGY

WHEN YOUR TABLE SPREAD IS DETERMINED BY THE FOODS grown, gathered, hunted, and raised, knowledge of the weather becomes a constant concern. Storms can ensure a meager winter, and drought, utter destruction. Knowing who and what to look to for answers about the weather has long been a way of Appalachian folks.

LORE FOR ALL SEASONS

WINTER

Winter in the mountains is a lean time. There are more
predictions for this season than any other. Some of these omens
are results of the laws of nature, and others, more mysterious.

Trees seem to have an uncanny ability to tell us of what is to
come. In Appalachia, there are many species of nuts: black
walnuts, acorns of all kinds, hickory nuts, and many more.
While today they are seen as a nuisance to some as they
pummel tin-roofed homes in autumn, they were once heavily
relied upon not just by squirrels, but by Appalachian people
as well.

Nut gathering and eating helped to provide valuable fat and
calories for the lean months of winter. The way the nut trees

produce can foretell what kind of winter is to come. It will be a bad winter if squirrels begin gathering nuts in early fall and their tails grow bushier. It will be a bad winter if hickory nuts have a heavy shell and if the pinecones open early. The dogwood, with blossoms as white as snow, also foretells a harsh winter if it is heavily laden with berries.

Just like the tails of the squirrels getting bushier, it is an omen of a harsh winter if the fur on the bottoms of a rabbit's feet grows in thick, as if they are putting on their winter boots. Birds also foretell harsh winters. It will be a bad winter if crows gather, and if screech owls sound like crying women. If birds are eating all the berries early, that too is a sure sign of a hard winter ahead. One of the most iconic animal omens of what the winter holds in store is the wooly worm. If the wooly worm is all black, the winter will be harsh; if one end is red, then that part of the winter will be mild. Crickets also sing of what is to come in winter. If you hear them clicking in the chimney, it is a sign of a harsh winter to come.

The months preceding the winter can also be observed to divine the winter's severity. There will be as many snows the following winter as there are rains in August. The sky and the moon can tell you as well: "Clear moon, frost soon." One of the most interesting winter predictions, however, is the idea of the "Ruling Days." These are the twelve days of Christmas, or December 25 through January 6. The weather observed on these twelve days can be used to determine the weather of the approaching year.

December 25 predicts the weather of January, December 26, February, and so on until you get to January 6. Write down the weather each day during the Ruling Days and see what is to come. Was it correct? You may be surprised.

Rain during the Ruling Days foretells a wet year, and a windy Christmas Day means the trees will bear much fruit. Any thunder during these days brings much snow the rest of winter. If it snows on Christmas night, the crops will do well. A clear, bright sun on Christmas day foretells a peaceful year and plenty. On Christmas Day, if ice hangs on the willow tree, the clover will be ready for harvest at Easter time.

SPRING

The traditions of spring in Appalachia foretell health and happiness after a long, dark winter. Spring tonic teas of spicebush twigs and sassafras roots bubble on the wood stove, chasing off the last of the chill. The groundhog was the harbinger of spring and announced winter's end on the second of February if he didn't see his shadow. This harkens back to much older pagan practices surrounding the ancient Irish holiday of Imbolc, where a black snake would foretell the same. If a thunderstorm arrived in March, it also meant an early spring. The whippoorwill calling and the beech tree leaves greening are the final signs that spring has settled in the mountains.

The rains of spring would determine the harvests of summer and autumn. If people wanted rain to come, they would kill a black snake and hang it up on a fence post. Today we know the black snake is a friend and eats rats and mice in plenty, so leave this as just a bit of lore. Fish will jump above the water to tell you rain is coming. Even your own hair serves as a rain omen. If your hair curls, expect rain.

"Evening red, morning gray, sets the traveler on his way; Evening gray, morning red, puts the traveler in his bed," and "Rain before seven, clear before eleven," are two common phrases traded in the mountains. Look to the sky to predict rain by more than just the clouds. If you see lightening in the north, it is a sign of dry weather to come. If you see the horns of the moon pointing downward, then it will surely rain in three days' time. If the fog lifts late, it will be a fine day.

SUMMER

Summer is the time of the dog star in Appalachia, when the constellation Sirius is overhead. There were many beliefs about the "dog days of summer," or July 3 through August 11, a time believed to be dangerous to people and animals. It was during these hottest of days when dogs and snakes were more likely to bite, and wounds wouldn't heal well. These days are called "dog days" because Sirius, the dog star, is ruling.

The black locust tree (*Robinia pseudoacacia*) is one of the common native and ever-useful trees of the Appalachians. In June they are laden with edible, fragrant white blossoms, much resembling a pea flower. When the locust blooms are heavy, it is a sign it will be a cool summer. If a cool August follows a hot July, it foretells a winter hard and dry. The wasps also seem to know when a dry summer is to come: they build their nests low when a dry summer approaches.

AUTUMN

The harvest time, one would assume, is the most ominous of all the seasons, yet is it always winter weather that has the most predictions. However, the autumn still has lore of its own.

When leaves fall early, fall and winter will be mild. If it is warm in October, it will be a cold February. If a full moon in October passes by without a frost, it is a sign that no frost will come until November's full moon. Christmastime was a useful time to look for omens, and it was said a clear star-filled night on Christmas Eve brought a hearty yield of crops in next year's harvest.

Though the dog days are past, in autumn the fear of fevers still loomed. To kill any caterpillar in summer is a sure way to get a fever before autumn's arrival. The chatterfly knows about autumn too, for fall is three months away when the first chatterfly chatters.

A SPELL TO BRING GOOD WEATHER

Repeat the following charm out loud three times when you see a ladybug:

"Ladybug, ladybug, fly away home,
Bring me good weather whenever you come."

To ensure good weather, place a hatchet in the yard or make a cross with matches and salt. This will surely charm the weather well.

PLANTING BY THE SIGNS WITH MOUNTAIN ASTROLOGY

Even humans in the earliest major civilizations, along the Nile and the Euphrates, used the moon's cycle to inform their farming practices. These planters may have believed that sowing their crops by the moon's phases or by the zodiac would increase their harvests while avoiding diseases and pests. In America, it was the German colonists who brought with them a long history of astrological omens, activities, and magical folk beliefs. Germans do not often come to mind in the general imagination of Appalachia, yet they are responsible for some of the strangest and most delightful aspects of folk magic in the mountains. As Appalachians mingled their cultures and bloodlines, German folk spiritual and cosmological beliefs were adopted by many others in the region.

One of the main ways that these astrological ideas were shared and recorded was the almanac. These publications were printed booklets of graphs, astrological information, calendars, and more, and were used for making weather predictions and deciding when to plant different crops, perform household tasks, and even cut one's hair. They were also used to spread and share occult information as well as folk healing practices and recipes.

PLANTING BY THE MOON

The moon has been the constant watcher of humanity since our beginning. The brilliant shining light illuminating the darkness that brought predators and marauders cast a benevolence upon us when we shivered in the night. The idea of planting in accordance with the moon phases is based upon the idea that the moon moves the tides and earthly water, so why not the water within a plant or seed?

First Quarter – The Moon Is Growing
(New Moon to First Quarter Moon)

During the first quarter of the moon, it is best to plant the following vegetables: asparagus, broccoli, brussels sprouts, barley, cabbage, cauliflower, celery, cucumbers, corn, cress, endive, kohlrabi, lettuce, leeks, oats, onions, parsley, and spinach, as well as seeds of flowering plants. However, avoid the first day of the full moon for planting and the days on which it changes quarters.

Second Quarter – The Moon Is Growing
(First Quarter Moon to Full Moon)

During the second quarter of the moon, it is best to plant beans, eggplant, muskmelon, peas (it is said that peas should be planted as near to noon as possible and some say that it is best to plant them on the new moon, though, as in all occult arts, opinions differ), peppers, pumpkin, squash, tomatoes, and watermelon. When possible, plant seed while the moon is in the most fruitful signs of Cancer, Scorpio, or Pisces. If that cannot be done, the next best signs are Taurus and Capricorn.

Third Quarter – The Moon Is Diminishing
(Full Moon to Last Quarter Moon)

During the third quarter of the moon, it is best to plant the following vegetables: artichoke, beets, carrots, chickory, parsnips, potatoes, radish, rutabaga, turnip, and all bulbous flowering plants.

Fourth Quarter – The Moon Is Diminishing
(Last Quarter Moon to New Moon)

During the fourth, or last, quarter of the moon, the tasks of life can be turned away from planting and focused upon other necessary work. Instead, prepare the soil, and then weed and deal with the plants' pests and diseases. These types of tasks, where the old or diseased growth is pruned out, are best done when the moon is in the barren signs of Gemini, Leo, and Virgo.

TIMING YOUR CROPS

In Appalachian tradition, it's essential to use the signs and moon phases to plant each crop at the right time. Here is some basic guidance for common crops:

+ Potatoes prefer to be planted when the signs are in the feet, at the new moon, a belief that comes from the German Appalachian tradition.

+ Corn does best when planted as the moon is becoming full, or better yet, when it is full.

+ Beets also love to be planted at the full of the moon, in the sign of Gemini or Cancer.

+ Beans prefer the full moon, and all the better if you plant them in new ground. The time of day can also be helpful in astrological planting, and beans prefer to be planted in the dark of night on Good Friday.

+ Cucumbers do best when planted at the last quarter of the new moon, especially in the sign of Gemini. If you plant them on the full moon, it is said they will be all runner vines and hardly any fruit.

+ Mustard greens and sweet potatoes, however, thrive if planted at the full moon.

+ Onions imitate the moon, for if the moon is just a sliver when they are planted, they will not root well and will come up out of the ground.

+ Peas are less picky and do best when planted the day after the full moon or the new moon, especially if the apple trees are in bloom.

+ Tomatoes do best on the second or third day after a full moon.

ASTROLOGICAL LORE

The heavens have long been observed by our ancestors and information about the mysteries of what is to come may be revealed there. Each place has its own astrological lore, and in the mountains there are many ways to look for meaning in the sky above.

THE NEW MOON

+ If you see the new moon, you may wish upon it and you'll see the face of your true love in your dreams.

New Moon new, this is the first time I have seen you,

I hope I may I hope I might,

See the one I love tonight.

If I am not his bride to be,

I hope his back be turned to me,

But if I am his body to embrace,

I hope to meet him face to face.

You may also wish upon the first star you see that night for a similar divination.

+ When you see a new moon enclose a star, it is a good night to make love.

+ The three days before and after the new moon are considered unlucky: one can say, "When there is no moon, there is no luck." However, you can change your luck by looking for the new moon over your right shoulder. Better yet, if you happen to glance at it without trying, and make a wish before speaking aloud, it will surely come true. But beware, some folks say it is bad luck to view the new moon over one's left shoulder.

✦ If you see the new moon between some trees, it can also bring bad luck, but you can combat it by shaking your dress at it. All the more reason to become familiar with the way the moon rises and sets in whatever holler you live in.

THE STARS

✦ For three nights in a row, gaze out your window and name three stars in the sky. Walk to your bed backwards and without speaking, and the person you dream of two nights out of the three will be your future betrothed. For seven nights in a row, count seven stars and the first person you shake hands with after this shall be your future mate.

✦ You can make wishes on stars as well. When you see the first star of the evening, you must ask someone three questions, all the while keeping your wish a secret. After three more days have come to pass, your wish will come true.

✦ You may also wish upon the first star you see by saying the following classic charm:

Star light, star bright, first star I see tonight,

I wish I may, I wish I might,

Have the wish I wish tonight.

* You can also wish on a shooting star as long as you get your wish out before the star disappears. But beware, because pointing at a shooting star is bad luck.

* In African folklore in Appalachia, it was bad luck to count the stars in general, for they could fall if you did, and bad luck as well to point at the moon.

* Stars can also be portents of danger. Shooting stars can be signs of a disaster, or even war. When the sky is lit and a meteor or comet passes amongst the stars, it is a sure sign of war to come. Comets can also signify strange or unusual events, as can eclipses.

RAINBOWS

* Rainbows are always special to see, and in Appalachia that is no exception. If there is a complete rainbow in times of global trouble, it means that war will end.

* A moon rainbow is especially rare, but to see one is a sure sign of good luck to come.

✻ SOME FINAL WORDS ✻

In popular culture, Appalachia is a place that seems to exist out of time. In reality, it is a region that is neither primitive nor nostalgic: it simply is. Appalachia holds the imagination of America for many reasons, but it deserves to be seen for the complex, beautiful, terrifying, and nuanced place that it is: a diverse and rich space, filled with songs, stories, and magic all its own. Appalachian folk magic is a microcosm of the story of America. A mixture of Indigenous, African, and European folk practices, forged into something entirely new in the foggy cauldron of the verdant mountains.

Folk practice is not static, and it is not frozen in time. We are writing it still. Whether you delve into this work from the perspective of trying to learn more about history or with the goal of incorporating this work into your own magical practice, it does not matter. We are living it now. The ways that Appalachian folk magic changes and adapts to our ever-evolving world will continue long after we are gone. This information is too precious, strange, and peculiar not to share and hold onto. While some practices are best let go of, others are deeply tied to long lineages of our ancestors' attempts to find meaning and control in an ultimately chaotic and wondrous world. Appalachian folk magic acts as a window for us, revealing the things most loved and most feared by peoples of the past. Perhaps not much has changed as we sit with those same feelings today.

⚛ BIBLIOGRAPHY ⚛

Anderson, Jeffrey E. *Conjure in African American Society*. Baton Rouge: Louisiana State University Press, 2007.

Bayard, S. P. "Witchcraft Magic and Spirits on the Border of Pennsylvania and West Virginia." *The Journal of American Folklore*, Vol. 51, No. 199 (Jan.–Mar., 1938), pp. 47–59.

Boughman, Arvis Locklear, and Oxendine, Loretta O. *Herbal remedies of the Lumbee Indians*. United Kingdom, McFarland, Incorporated, Publishers, 2004. p. 74.

Butler, Jon. "Magic, Astrology, and the Early American Religious Heritage, 1600-1760." The American Historical Review, 84, no. 2, 1979, p. 317.

Cavender, Anthony. "Folk Hematology in the Appalachian South." *Journal of Folklore* Research, 1992. 23.

Cavender, A. "Folk medical uses of plant foods in southern Appalachia, United States." Journal of Ethnopharmacology 108, (January 1, 2006): 74–84.

Cavender, Anthony P. *Folk Medicine in Southern Appalachia*. Chapel Hill: University of North Carolina Press, 2003.

Chadwell, J. Tyler and Tiffany D. Martin. "Mountain Mystics: Magic Practitioners in Appalachian Witchlore." *Bulletin of the Transilvania University of Brasov, Series IV:*

Philology & Cultural Studies, vol. 9, no. 1, Jan. 2016, pp. 49–56.

Chisholm, Hugh, ed. "Hellebore". Encyclopædia Britannica. 13 (11th ed.). Cambridge University Press. 1910.

"Conjuring and Conjure-Doctors in the Southern United States (Continued)." The Journal of American Folklore, vol. 9, no. 34, July 1896, p. 224.

Combs, Josiah Henry. "Sympathetic Magic in the Kentucky Mountains: Some Curious Folk-Survivals." *The Journal of American Folklore*, vol. 27, no. 105, 1914, pp. 328–330.

Covey, Herbert C. *African-American Slave Medicine: Herbal and non-Herbal Treatments*. United Kingdom, Lexington Books, 2007. p.133.

Crellin J, K. *Trying to Give Ease Tommie Bass and the Story of Herbal Medicine*. Duke University Press, 1997. p. 166.

Davis, Donald E. *Southern United States: an Environmental History*. ABC-CLIO, 2006.

Davis, Hubert J. *American Witch Stories*. Middle Village, N.Y. : Jonathan David Publishers, 1990.

Dawley, Katy. "The Campaign to Eliminate the Midwife," *American Journal of Nursing* 100 (October 2000): 50.

Eisenstadt, Peter. "Almanacs and the Disenchantment of Early America." *Pennsylvania History: A Journal of Mid-Atlantic Studies*, vol. 65, no. 2, 1998, p. 143.

Elliott, Douglas B. *Wild Roots: A Forager's Guide to the Edible and Medicinal Roots, Tubers, Corms, and Rhizomes of North America*. Rochester, VT: Healing Arts, 1995.

Gainer, Patrick W., Judy Prozzillo Byers, and Muse Project. *Witches, Ghosts, And Signs: Folklore Of The Southern Appalachians*. Morgantown: Vandalia Press, 2008.

Hatfield, Gabrielle. *Encyclopedia of Folk Medicine: Old World and New World Traditions*. Santa Barbara, Calif.: ABC-CLIO, 2004.

Kerrigan, William. "Apples on the Border: Orchards and the Contest for the Great Lakes." *Michigan Historical Review*, vol. 34, no. 1, 2008, pp. 25–41.

Kilpatrick, Alan. *The Night Has a Naked Soul. Witchcraft and Sorcery among the Western Cherokee*. Syracuse NY: Syracuse University Press, 1997.

Kingsbury, S. "For the love of sassafras." Journal Of The American Herbalists Guild 9, no. 1 (March 2009): 24–30.

Krochmal, Arnold. "Medicinal Plants and Appalachia." *Economic Botany*, vol. 22, no. 4, 1968, pp. 332–337. *JSTOR*, JSTOR, www.jstor.org/stable/4252992.

Light, PD. "A History of Southern and Appalachian Folk Medicine." Journal Of the American Herbalists Guild 8, no. 2 (September 2008): 27–38. (27)

Milnes, Gerald. *Signs, Cures, & Witchery : German Appalachian Folklore*. Knoxville: University of Tennessee Press, 2007. 91–108.

Mitchell, Faith. *Hoodoo Medicine : Gullah herbal remedies*. Colombia, Summerhouse Press, 1998. p. 70.

Moerman, Daniel E. *Native American Ethnobotany*. United States, Timber Press, 1998. p. 250

Moldenke, Harold N. and Alma L. Moldenke. *Plants of the Bible*. New York, NY: The Ronald Press Company, 1952.

Netter, M. W. "The Mandrake Medical Superstition." The Medical Standard. Vol. III. Chicago: G.P. Englehard, 1888. 173–75.

Nikolas Monardes. *Joyful News Out of the New- found World*. Translated by John Frampton, London: Printed by E. Aide by the assign of Bonham Norton, 1596.

Patton, Darryl. *Mountain Medicine: The Herbal Remedies of Tommie Bass*. United States, Natural Reader Press, 2004.

Persons, W. Scott, and J. M. Davis. *Growing & Marketing Ginseng, Goldenseal & Other Woodland Medicinals*. Fairview, NC: Bright Mountain, 2005.

Raedisch, Linda. *Night of the Witches: Folklore, Traditions & Recipes for Celebrating Walpurgis Night*. Woodbury, MN: Llewellyn Publications, 2011.

Rätsch Christian. *The Encyclopedia of Psychoactive Plants: Ethnopharmacology and Its Applications*. Park Street Press, 2005.

Rehder, John B. *Appalachian Folkways*. Baltimore: Johns Hopkins University Press, 2004.

Rupp, Rebecca. *Red Oaks & Black Birches: The Science and Lore of Trees*. Pownal, VT: Storey Communications, 1990.

Rush, John A. *Entheogens and the Development of Culture: The Anthropology and Neurobiology of Ecstatic Experience: Essays*. California, 2013.

Sanders, Jack. *The Secrets of Wildflowers: A Delightful Feast of Little-Known Facts, Folklore, and History*. Guilford, CT: Lyons, 2003.

Schwartz, James, and Scott A Norton. "Useful plants of dermatology. VI. The mayapple (Podophyllum)." Journal Of the American Academy Of Dermatology 47, no. 5 (November 2002): 774–775.

Tantaquidgeon, Gladys. "Mohegan Medicinal Practices, Weatherlore and Superstitions." Smithsonian Institution- Bureau of Ethnology Annual Report 44 (1928): 264-70.

Thomas, Daniel Lindsey, and Lucy Blayney Thomas. *Kentucky Superstitions*. Princeton, Princeton University Press, 1920. #2993.

Vance, Randolph. *Ozark Magic and Folklore*. New York, NY: Dover Publications, 1964, c. 1947.

Weston, Brandon. *Asateotida*. Ozark Healing Traditions. Web. https://www.ozarkhealing.com/asafetida.html

White, Newman Ivey, and Frank Clyde Brown. *The Frank C. Brown Collection of North Carolina Folklore; the Folklore of North Carolina*. Durham: Duke University Press [1952–64], 1952.

Wigginton, Eliot. *Foxfire 4 Water Systems, Fiddle Making, Logging, Gardening, Sassafras Tea, Wood Carving, and Further Affairs of Plain Living*. Garden City: Anchor, 1977.

Willard, Fred L., Victor G. Aeby, and Tracy Carpenter-Aeby. "Sassafras in the New World and the Syphilis Exchange." *Journal Of Instructional Psychology* 41, no. 1–4 (March 2014): 3–9.

Yronwode, Catherine. *Hoodoo Herb and Root Magic: A Materia Magica of African-American Conjure*. Lucky Mojo Curio Company: Root Doctor, 2002.

Vogt, Evon Z., and Peggy Golde. "Some Aspects of the Folklore of Water Witching in the United States." The Journal of American Folklore, vol. 71, no. 282, 1958, pp. 519–531. JSTOR, www.jstor.org/stable/537458. Accessed 3 Aug. 2020.

⚝ INDEX ⚝

ACKNOWLEDGMENTS

Thank you to these mountains for holding me; my partners, Corby and Adrianna, for loving me; my best friends Saro, Baylen, John, and Liam for their undying support and deep love of the Old Ways. Thank you to my brothers for supporting their wild sister even if sometimes I am hard to understand, and most importantly, thank you to the Appalachian people—the Indigenous, Black, and working-class peoples of these beloved mountains—for their unique contributions and creations in this vibrant and complex folk culture.

ABOUT THE AUTHOR

REBECCA BEYER is an Appalachian ethnobotanist living in the mountains of Western North Carolina, where she manages a homestead and teaches traditional witchcraft, foraging, and Appalachian folk medicine. She has a BS in plant and soil science from the University of Vermont and a master's in Appalachian studies and sustainability, concentrating in Appalachian ethnobotany, from Appalachian State University. She is also a member of the Association of Foragers. She spends her days trying to learn what her ancestors did and finding ways to share traditional skills while tackling cultural appropriation and the complexities of living in the modern world.